MORAL QUESTIONS

Moral Questions

by
James Gaffney

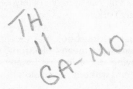

PAULIST PRESS
New York / Paramus / Toronto

The chapters in this book originally appeared in *Service*, Vol. 1, copyright © 1973, 1974 by The Missionary Society of St. Paul the Apostle in the State of New York.

Library of Congress
Catalog Card Number: 74-30536

ISBN: 0-8091-1870-X

COVER DESIGN: Gloria Ortiz

Published by Paulist Press
Editorial Office: 1865 Broadway, N.Y., N.Y. 10023
Business Office: 400 Sette Drive, Paramus, N.J. 07652

Printed and bound in the
United States of America

Contents

Introduction   1

1. Contextual Ethics and the "New Morality"   5

2. Changing Perspectives in Sexual Morality   16

3. Respect for Life: The Abortion Controversy   28

4. The Christian Family: The Domestic Church   39

5. What God Has Joined   50

6. The Persistence of Samaritans   61

7. Drugs: The Choice and the Alternatives   72

8. Honesty: A Name for Many Virtues   83

9. Perverted, Queer, or Gay?   95

10. Societies as Sinners   106

11. The Sacrament Called Penance   117

12. Growing Up Moral   129

Suggested Readings   141

To
Kathleen

"When two upon a journey go, one sees
before the other."

Introduction

"In ethical matters, absolute certainty is very difficult to attain," said Aristotle in his *Nichomachean Ethics*, and, more than a score of centuries later, his opinion seems to be widely shared even among Catholics.

I say *even* among Catholics, because it would appear that if there was ever a major body of opinion that might take issue with Aristotle's moderate diffidence, it was to be found, until very recently, in the Roman Catholic Church. Many readers will doubtless remember the celebrated "question box" sessions which were once an indispensable feature of Catholic spiritual retreats. Out of a box were drawn, one after another, unsigned slips of paper bearing questions about right and wrong behavior, no less remarkable for the richness of their variety than for the fineness of their detail. And one after another, those questions were *answered*. Never was the answer a disclaimer of knowledge or competence to decide. Never was the answer introduced by a "maybe" or "probably" or other formula of uncertainty. And rarely was the answer questioned or challenged, unless by the introduction of finer distinctions or more complicating circumstances, which were thereupon no less summarily disposed of. Very few thought of the procedure as either arrogant or absurd. For among Catholics it was widely

1

assumed that, to practical moral questions, these priests really did know all the answers, because they got their answers—somehow—from the Church, and the Church got them—somehow—from God.

Those who were privileged to look more deeply into this system's rationale acquired a more sophisticated understanding of it. The Church was divinely constituted as "custodian of both the natural and the revealed law." All moral questions resided in one or the other of those two realms of law. Correct answers to those questions were the prerogative of custodianship, guaranteed by God's enlightenment to the Church's magisterium, at the summit of which stood the pope, whose infallibility could, in principle, resolve any doubts, and around the base of which were ranged the moral theologians, whose "opinions," as approved at least tacitly by their hierarchical superiors, furnished a great arsenal of moral assurances. It was for the most part these ecclesiastically endorsed opinions which were invoked to answer questions, whether from question boxes or in confessional boxes or wherever else the moral perplexities of Catholics came to light.

Times have changed. And recent times have brought rapid and drastic changes to the moral thinking of Catholics. At the last annual convention of the Catholic Theological Society of America the question assigned to moral theology was whether or not there is a distinctive Catholic or even Christian ethic. The principal speaker, a priest who is perhaps at the moment America's best known Catholic moral theologian, answered that question with a decided negative, on the grounds that among Catholics and Christians moral views vary just about as widely as among the general population. Although the first respondent, a distinguished Protestant theologian, offered serious objections to that answer, there was certainly nothing remotely like an outcry of protest from an overwhelmingly Catholic and clerical audience of professional theologians.

Again, in each of the past two years, American Catholicism's most widely respected theological journal, *Theological Studies*, carried articles under the title "Infallibility in Morals." The earlier of them concludes that the Church cannot so define a moral doctrine as to provide that the content of that doctrine will remain permanently irreformable—but also contends that this conclusion does not conflict with the dogma of infallibility. The later article, while admitting the plausibility of that conclusion, considers the contention that it does not conflict with the dogma of infallibility to be indefensible.

I cite these examples from highly respected sources of American Catholic theological opinion in order to emphasize that the contrast between present and past modes of thinking in Catholic morality is not a phenomenon restricted to amateurs, sensationalists, and upstarts. It is a contrast which is evident over the entire field of Catholic ethics, and which affects methodology no less deeply than conclusions. At every level, Catholic moral answers are being questioned.

And yet at the same time, Catholic moral questions

continue to be asked and deserve to be answered. It remains the obligation of every Catholic moral teacher, from parent to pope, to answer them as truly and helpfully as he can. The great majority of them cannot be answered as simply or as confidently as before, nor can official answers be as sure of agreement as once they were.

The following pages represent a very modest contribution toward the answering of some questions which were presented to—not selected by—the present author. The questions, which were originally harvested by the publisher, take the form of rather general topics which representative groups of Catholic clergy expressed special interest in having discussed with a convenient degree of brevity. The requirement of brevity made it necessary to leave out a great deal—of argumentation, illustration, and elaboration—which would be indispensable to a scholarly presentation. Despite this defect, which is no inconsiderable one, the essays are collected here in the belief that such brevity may be a service to other readers, whose circumstances make more extensive reading about so many different topics impracticable, and who may share with me the view of Gilbert Keith Chesterton, that if a thing is worth doing, it is worth doing even rather badly.

Chapter 1

Contextual Ethics and the "New Morality"

A good many years ago American audiences were amused by a current popular comedy entitled *Nothing But the Truth*. It was the kind of story that almost writes itself once a competent author is fortunate enough to hit on the initial idea. In this case, the initial idea was the very simple, familiar, and commonly accepted moral generalization that people ought to tell the truth and not tell lies. The comic heroine of the play was a well-meaning, strong-willed, weak-witted lady who, in a fit of moral fervor, self-righteously resolved to abide by that moral principle with inflexible firmness. She kept her resolution, with results that are easy enough to imagine. Having decided to say, in any and all circumstances, only what she believed to be strictly true, her conversation quickly became an intolerable source of boredom, embarrassment, misunderstanding, and offense for everyone around her, and made an angry, aggrieved chaos out of every social situation she became involved in. Ultimately, the evil consequences of her "good" resolution became too much even for her. She was reconverted to the obviously wiser and kinder ethical policy of being less absolute and more discriminating in the delicate matter of telling the truth.

The conversion that ended that comedy, together with the series of social disasters that made it comic, was, strictly speaking, a conversion to contextual ethics. It so happened that the particular example selected was of a kind of contextual ethics that everybody with common sense and social experience has been practicing, almost without thinking about it, from time immemorial. The result was that audiences could enjoy all the incongruities and absurdities with a comfortable sense of superiority, and without having reason to suspect that their own moral convictions or practices were being criticized, ridiculed, or threatened.

For all of us learn during our most impressionable years that telling the family visitor with a bizarre dress or funny face exactly what she looks like is not accorded the same moral honors as George Washington's frankness about the cherry tree. And similar lessons throughout the rest of life teach us that plain, unvarnished truth is by no means always what the best in human behavior seems to call for. As a result, normally good, conscientious people find themselves with a general principle, "Tell the truth," or "Don't tell lies," which they also recognize as an oversimplification allowing plenty of important exceptions. About all those exceptions it is very difficult to generalize, but experience teaches us that usually, though by no means always, they can be recognized without too much trouble when appropriate situations arise. Students of Catholic moral theology may recall that older textbook writers tried valiantly to redefine "lying" in such a way as to exclude all those situations in which it is obviously a good thing not to tell the truth, the whole truth, and nothing but the truth. Unfortunately, their results were neither very helpful nor very uniform.

Why did those moral theologians burden themselves with so thankless and apparently fruitless a task as finding a subtler definition of lying than the traditional *locutio contra mentem*, "saying what you don't think"? Clearly enough, they did so because what they were trying to achieve was what we might call an "air-tight system," a moral theology free of loopholes. And no wonder. For they considered their own vocation to be one of serving the Church by articulating as perfectly as possible and applying as practically as possible the "law" of God, whether "natural" or "revealed." And if good laws, even of the merely man-made kind, are expected to avoid loopholes, how much less ought loopholes to be tolerated in formulating the laws of God? Consequently, they tried out their countless different definitions of *mendacium* in a fading hope of at last hitting upon one that would make it possible to set down "Thou shalt not lie" as a law of God that meant just what the words said, with no ifs, ands, or buts. If they succeeded, the Christian would henceforth be spared the complex mental problem of deciding when he should and when he should not lie, and left with the far simpler one of merely recognizing a lie, as defined by the experts, when he saw one.

In our discussion so far, we have seen three distinct approaches to the ethics of truth-telling. The first approach, represented by the character in the play, is to take a rough and ready generalization of popular morality and follow it literally, as an absolute norm of behavior. This is in spite of the fact that to do so leads to all sorts of behavior that obviously violates other, no less respectable moral values, especially in the area of sympathetic kindness and sensitive consideration for others.

The second approach, represented by the authors of moral treatises investigating the nature of lying, is to recognize that the general principle is one that does not exclude all exceptions, and then try to rephrase the principle or redefine its terms in such a way that legitimate exceptions will be effectively excluded.

The last approach is that of the great majority of people whose approach to moral questions is neither fanatical, like that of the character in the play, nor technical, like that of the textbook writers, but is nevertheless intelligent and earnest. And it is, as I have said, precisely the approach of contextual ethics. If it were restricted to such matters as lying, it would undoubtedly receive a lot less publicity, and provoke a lot less interest and, in some quarters, indignation. But, for good or ill, it is an approach that more and more people, including Catholics, have been applying more and more widely. Most of the enthusiasm, as well as most of the scandal currently associated with contextual ethics and the "new morality" for which it is praised and blamed, originates at the point where it is applied to more sensitive principles, notably in the area of sexual morality.

Controversial attitudes on the part of modern Catholics toward sexual morality will be the subject of the next article in this series. But a certain amount of insight into controversial modern approaches to morality in general can be gained by comparing the contextual ethics that has long been taken for granted in the case of lying, with the contextual ethics that provokes so much controversy when it is applied to sexual behavior. For the way most Catholics have always treated the moral prohibition "Thou shalt not lie" is precisely the way increasingly many Catholics now treat such moral prohibitions as "Thou shalt not fornicate." And, as a matter of fact, what most people mean by "the new morality" amounts to very little more than applying that same approach to all moral prohibitions without exception.

In order to understand and evaluate that approach, let us begin by considering some of the situations in which most conscientious people would certainly agree that it is better to tell an untruth, whether you call it a lie or some more inoffensive name, than to tell the truth. Good people most frequently justify not telling the truth when they are trying to spare other people some needless trouble, danger, or distress, or to give them some innocent pleasure or encouragement. Thus, a wife may tell her family she feels fine even when she is feeling miserable, in order to spare them worry. Or a husband may tell his wife she looks beautiful when despite her best efforts she does not, simply to cheer her up. Or a man may deny reports which he knows to be true when they serve no good purpose, but could seriously damage the reputation or endanger the position of another. When the bishop in *Les Miserables* tells the police that the thief they have just caught running away with his silverware was actually his guest to whom he had given the silver as a present, we scarcely regard the lie as detracting from the bishop's Christian character.

Similar examples could be multiplied endlessly. However much we might quibble over details, we could certainly find a very large measure of agreement, among people who take morality seriously, in admitting lots of occasions when it is really a better thing to tell an untruth than to be strictly truthful. To borrow a useful bit of terminology from Mark Twain, not all lies are "damned lies." And if we examine and compare examples of what we can agree are morally good falsifications, I think we shall find that most if not all of them earn our moral approval by fulfilling the same two conditions. First, they do not do serious harm to anybody. And second, they are acts of human kindness or Christian charity, that is, acts which benefit others. To put it briefly, they are harmless, generous, helpful acts. "Damned lies" are selfish, damaging, irresponsible acts.

What defenders of the so-called "new morality" based on contextual ethics wish to imply is that our moral prohibition of lying is not a peculiar kind of moral principle, but a perfectly typical one. As we understand it in practice, what that principle means is that to be untruthful in our use of words is something that is *usually* evil. This, therefore, we should be careful to avoid, *except* in those relatively *unusual situations* where by telling an untruth we act more *responsibly* and *generously*, in a way that confers real benefit on somebody, and does no real harm to anybody.

Now if we take that description of the moral principle about lying as a model for understanding moral principles generally, two main characteristics of the "new morality" will appear quite clearly. In the first place, sound moral principles do not state what is *always* the case, *without any exception*, but rather what is *usually* the case, *with certain exceptions*. And in the second place, the main test of whether or not a particular situation represents an exception to an accepted moral principle is whether or not by acting contrary to that principle one is acting in a *more responsible and generous* manner than he would be if he followed it literally.

One of the things that advocates of contextual ethics are sometimes criticized for is naive optimism. But while there may be something to that criticism, I think it is clear enough at this point that advocates of the "new morality" are in one way more optimistic but in another way decidedly more pessimistic about human moralizing than their more conservative predecessors. They are more pessimistic about man's ability to express his moral convictions in generalizations so perfect that they will anticipate and provide for every possible relevant situation. They are pessimistic, in other words, about the capacity of human foresight and human lan-

guage. On the other hand, what they are more optimistic about is man's ability to respond to the peculiar moral requirements of particular
circumstances and to recognize what is the generous and constructive way to behave in a given situation. In other words, they are more optimistic about
the capacity of human insight and human conscience.

Throughout this discussion, I have reluctantly
adopted the expression "new morality" because it is
a bit of jargon which contemporary writers have
made it impossible to ignore and almost impossible
to avoid, apparently on the assumption that with
ethics as with detergents and breakfast cereals you
can't get modern people interested in anything
unless you advertise it as "new." I have persisted in
putting quotation marks around "new morality" as a
reminder that I consider it a misleading expression,
and one that I should be happy to hear the last of.
For there is nothing in the least new about the kind
of approach to moral generalizations we have been
describing. We have already seen that it has always
been, for Catholics no less than for others, the kind
of approach good people normally take to the general prohibition against lying. (And it may be relevant to recall that among the ten commandments
what we find is not a condemnation of lying in general, but a much more contextual prohibition,
against doing harm to other people by submitting
false testimony about them.) Nor is the "old" morality really terribly different in its approach to ethical questions other than lying. Take for example
such a crucial and venerable prohibition as "Thou

shalt not kill." Obviously, this principle too has to be qualified in innumerable ways to accommodate the moral requirements of different situations. Everyone will agree readily enough to the generalization "Thou shalt not kill," but, even among Catholics, how far does that agreement go when it comes to applying the generalization to questions about killing, for example, criminals convicted of capital offenses, or enemy soldiers in undeclared or morally ambiguous wars, or unborn embryos conceived through violence or folly? Good people, good Catholics, good philosophers, and good theologians, of the present age and of all preceding ages, can be cited on both sides of these and countless other questions about the rights and wrongs not only of killing, but of most other general categories of moral behavior.

The main influence of contextual ethics consists in encouraging us to think of our moral generalizations as being much more similar to what we mean by maxims than to what we mean by laws. That is, they are summary statements of a consensus of human wisdom applied to specific areas of ethical behavior, and as such they are indispensable guides to living a life consistent with such wisdom. But it remains true that the concrete circumstances of human life are too subtly complicated and unpredictably changing to be completely circumscribed by any moral abstractions. It is the duty of responsible adults to make their moral decisions in the light of sound ethical maxims, but not by slavish, unreflective reliance on them.

When such maxims are found to be too simple for
the complexities of a given situation, a man is not
left to follow personal whims or local fashions.
Rather, as the Second Vatican Council reminded us,
"in the depths of his conscience man detects a law
which he does not impose upon himself, but which
holds him to obedience. Always summoning him to
love good and avoid evil, the voice of conscience
can when necessary speak to his heart more specifically: do this, shun that. For man has in his heart a
law written by God" (*Gaudium et Spes*, n. 16). Since
it is the glory of a Christian's morality to realize that
that law is the law of love, it natural that contemporary Christian moralists should emphasize love as
the supreme norm for all good moral behavior. Indeed, the Council itself immediately adds, "In a
wonderful manner conscience reveals that law
which is fulfilled by love of God and neighbor."

Unfortunately, however, love has become for our
civilization so extremely ambiguous a word that it
frequently stands for motives and values that are irrelevant or even contrary to Christian charity. Au-
gustine's saying, "Love and do what you wish," so
often quoted by contemporary moralists, does indeed epitomize the whole of Christian ethics. But it
only does so as long as the love we are talking about
is the kind of love that can be fittingly symbolized by
no gentler or more sentimental image than that of
God incarnate nailed to a cross. Christian defenders
of contextual ethics act most irresponsibly when,
claiming to speak in the name of Jesus Christ, they
simply proclaim that all morality comes down to loving one another. Jesus did not do anything so silly or

so dangerous as telling his followers that all they had to do was love one another. What he said was "Love one another as I have loved you," and he both clearly explained and vividly demonstrated precisely what that meant. No morality based on a lesser kind of love than that can claim to be Christian morality. And quite a lot of behavior that is based on lesser kinds of love cannot claim to be morality at all.

Chapter 2

Changing Perspectives in Sexual Morality

An interesting question to ask oneself in the climate of controversy that currently surrounds Catholic morality is to what extent two Catholics, one following the guidance of traditional moral theology and the other adopting the approach of modern contextual ethics, would be led to significantly different practical conclusions about various moral questions. My own impression is that in most areas of morality the practical conclusions they arrive at would be decidedly similar.

In one area of morality, however, I have to admit that I cannot imagine how a contextual approach could lead to anything remotely like the conclusions imposed on Catholics by traditional moral theology. That area is the realm of sexual morality, and it has been my impression that critics who show the most intense hostility toward contextual ethics, as well as those who are most enthusiastically in favor of it, usually have issues of sexual morality uppermost in their minds. This fact alone might lead us to suspect that there is something quite peculiar about Catholic sexual ethics, and a closer examination leaves no doubt that there is.

It used to be a fairly common experience of Catholic priests in administering the sacrament of penance to children barely out of infancy to hear some piping voice of uncertain gender proclaim "I committed adultery," adding a number of times for the offense which sometimes reached three figures. Inquiries into the details of these prodigies of precocious lust usually elicited such clarifications as a little girl's admission of having "peeed in the bushes" or a little boy's of having "played with my thing." It was all very amusing, and helped both to enliven a dull job and to contribute to the aura of "oh-so-cuteness" that was long a cherished feature of American Catholicism's self-image.

Underlying the comic relief, however, was a fact whose implications are more serious. For the children's misunderstandings were clearly the result of a kind of instruction and innuendo that lumped together every disapproved-of act or attitude involving the urino-genital system as behavior denounced in thunder by God on Sinai. For many Catholics, I am sure, the precise meaning of the word adultery has never fully replaced its earlier connotation of a vast, indiscriminate realm of things that were sexy, "dirty," and bad.

In churches no less than in families, what is on the lips of the children interestingly reflects what is on the minds of adults. And among Catholics, the chil-

dren's ludicrously broad conception of "adultery"
reflected a rather extraordinary aspect of their
Church's moral theology. The most glaring manifestation that occurs to me of this peculiarity of Catholic sexual teaching is the doctrine traditionally stated
as *"non datur parvitas materiae in re venerea."* According to this doctrine, which enjoyed such strong
official support that it has only recently been criticized in books bearing an *imprimatur,* no sexual
misbehavior, no matter how seemingly trivial, could
be other than grievous matter, and if it did not constitute mortal sin it could only be for lack of sufficient reflection or full consent of the will.

As a result, the adolescent masturbator trying to
banish depression with erotic daydreams, the infa-
tuated lover fumbling around the periphery of his
girl-friend's bra, the unscrupulous career girl earn-
ing overtime in her bosses' beds, and the sadistic
rapist lying in ambush for school children, all took
their places in Catholic imagination side by side on
the brink of hell. Sex, any kind of sex, assumed for
Catholics an ominous importance which non-
Catholics found difficult to comprehend and ex-
Catholics found difficult to forgive, and accounted
for an extraordinary proportion of the time spent by
Catholic priests and teachers in counseling and exhortation.

This rather grim view of the sinful potentialities of
sex derived from a theoretical starting point that
gave it a certain logical consistency. That starting
point was the conviction that sexual activities, the
sexual organs that serve them, the sexual emotions

that accompany them, and the sexual stimuli that motivate them are all naturally directed to sexual intercourse, whose intrinsic purpose is the procreation of children, and whose only legitimate setting is in marriage, the primary purpose of which is the generation and upbringing of children. Consequently, outside of marriage all sex was wrong, while inside marriage all sex was right as long as it was not inconsistent with the goal of bearing and rearing offspring. The further doctrine that when sex was wrong, it was always, at least objectively, gravely wrong, was based on the same idea that all sexual behavior is ordered to the same purpose, which, if it does not serve, it frustrates. The seriousness of the fault in sexual sin derives from the seriousness of the purpose it frustrates: the generation and upbringing of children, on which the very future of humanity depends.

Given the traditional Catholic analysis of sexual morality, all sexual behavior was judged according to whether or not it was oriented toward the sexual intercourse of husband and wife, and thereby toward the generation and upbringing of children. If not, it was considered to be objectively a grave fault, and all that remained was to determine whether in particular cases subjective factors might lessen the individual's guilt. The fundamental idea on which this whole analysis rests is the idea that *we know what sex is for* and what it is for is *having and raising children.*

What recent approaches to sexual morality mainly disagree about is not so much how to answer the

question "What is sex for?" but whether or not it is
really a good idea to make any answer to that question a general norm for sexual morality. For it certainly seems to be true that in most moral questions
we are not so much interested in the abstract purpose we attribute to some *thing* (like the physical act
of intercourse) as in the concrete motive we ascribe
to some *person* (like a husband or wife or lover)
who uses or does the thing.

And after all, it is not very easy to specify the purpose of any *thing* apart from the intelligent purposes of persons who use it. The man who invented
the saw probably thought only of woodcutting, but
that does not alter the fact that some people use
saws only for playing tunes. It may seem obvious to
say that God made our eyes for seeing, but anyone
who has been gazed at with love or glared at with
hatred knows that eyes also serve very well for *saying* certain things. And if eating food were allowed
no purpose but the strictly biological one of nutri-
tion, most of us would have to change drastically
both our menus and our social lives. By the same
token, one may question whether it is more enlight-
ening to ask what sex is for, or to ask instead what
certain human beings perform certain sexual acts
for. If we find that human beings perform sexual
acts for what seem to be good purposes, and
achieve results which correspond to those good
purposes, without producing bad effects which out-
weigh the good, it may not seem altogether reasonable to condemn their behavior because it was
not done for some other purpose instead. But it
should be realized that to admit only that much

opens the way to a basically contextual approach to sexual morality.

The contextual attitude toward sexual morals, which many Christians, especially young ones, now tend to adopt as enlightened and wholesome, considers sex as one of the many resources which God has given us without attaching a sheet of instructions headed "use only as directed." Rather, God expects us to apply our intelligence and experience to discover how it can best be used in the loving service of God and our neighbor. Here again, the moral value of our conduct is to be determined by whether or not it can really be called generous and responsible conduct, the only kind of conduct worthy of a Christian, whose life is meant to be based on the love revealed in Jesus Christ.

Modern Christians are quick to remind us, however, that what constitutes generous and responsible behavior depends on variable circumstances, and that relevant circumstances can change dramatically over the course of time. Thus, for example, it is readily admitted that it would be ungenerous and irresponsible to seek or give sexual gratification at the risk of causing illegitimate pregnancy or of transmitting venereal disease. But once such risks have been virtually eliminated by technological progress, one has to answer the moral question on other grounds, of a more personal, social, and psychological nature. Thus, defenders of a new sexual morality do not necessarily suppose that the sexual morality of previous generations was wrong or foolish. In circumstances that formerly prevailed, there was excellent reason, even in terms of situation ethics, to oppose extra-marital sex, for without modern resources of contraception and prophylaxis, such behavior could seldom be considered generous and responsible. True to its name, contextual ethics maintains that sexual morality should change because, as a matter of fact, the situation has changed. On the other hand, a more conservative school of Catholic moralists maintains that sexual morality should not change because the supposedly God-given purpose of sexuality has not changed. Recent literature makes it quite clear that at the present time both of these schools of thought are well-represented in the Catholic Church, among not only its laity, but also its clergy, theologians, and hierarchy.

While it would be hard to establish which school of thought currently represents a majority, I think it is easy to see which represents the predominant trend. There is no mistaking the increasingly contextual trend in recent books of Catholic theology, in lectures and discussions taking place on Catholic campuses, and in the thoughtful conversations of Catholic people generally. And even on the most conservative level of official Church teaching, this trend has drawn encouragement from the Second Vatican Council's modified presentation of the ends of matrimony (*Gaudium et Spes,* 50), and from concessions and uncertainties in the area of papal teaching with regard to contraception. Lack of space compels me to rely on a bibliographical reference to demonstrate the evolution and flexibility of Catholic doctrine in this area, in order to devote the remainder of this discussion to considering some of the factors that might be kept in mind when evaluating sexual behavior from a more contextual viewpoint. Moreover, since this book contains separate chapters on abortion, contraception, divorce, and homosexuality, the main subject to be treated here will be that of extra-marital sex.

Critics of the traditional Christian ban against all extra-marital intercourse, considered as fornication, are undoubtedly justified in saying that good reasons for upholding that prohibition have been deprived of much of their force by advances in contraceptive technology. On the other hand, it is a well-documented fact that during recent years, despite the efficiency and availability of safeguards, our own country has seen an unprecedented increase both of venereal disease and of unmarried pregnancies, the latter contributing in turn to ever more frequent abortions. These facts alone are sufficient to indicate that a great many cases of extra-marital intercourse cannot make the most minimal claim of being generous and responsible conduct motivated by Christian love. My own experience of counseling, teaching, and living very closely with Catholic college students leaves me no doubt that in this area young Catholics, whom I liked and admired, frequently failed to practice the sexual morality that they themselves preached. Much of what is currently written about the sex life of young Catholics betrays a naive romanticism in its failure to recognize that a considerable portion of it is crudely selfish and cruelly insensitive. Plain, old-fashioned lust, even among verbally idealistic youth, remains a commonplace reality, and one on which the judgment of a morality based on generosity, responsibility, and Christian love can only be scathingly severe. The problem in this connection, which I believe is a grave one, is not with the "new morality" at all. It is with a *new sentimentality,* not uncommon among counselors and clergy, which seems to imagine that all the extra-marital intercourse of contemporary youth is modeled on the idyllic embraces of *Love Story.* The moralist, counselor, or confessor, who does not see or cannot believe that unreflective passion and calculating seduction, often facilitated by chemical stimulation and a cultural barrage of popular obscenity, still account for a great deal of extra-marital intercourse, is an extremely dangerous kind of fool. If the love-centered ethic of the "new morality" is to be our standard for evaluating human conduct, it must be applied with clear-sighted honesty. And if it corresponds as closely to the Word of God as it claims to do, we should not be surprised to find it a two-edged sword.

Closely related to this romantic inability to recognize obvious abuses of sex is a tendency to overrate the moral value of sex. Again and again in reading current Catholic literature by clergy and theologians, one finds statements to the effect that intercourse is the "deepest," or "richest," or "fullest" expression of the "deepest," or "richest," or "fullest" love man can achieve. While it is unquestionable that intercourse can beautifully express an immensity of love, it also can, and often does, fall greatly short of the accomplishment. But what is more important is to ask how such unqualified superlatives about the kind of love expressed in sex can win the unquestioning approval of Christians, who profess to believe that the perfection of love is revealed to us in a man of whose sex life we know nothing, and whose love had its climax not in the sweet reciprocity of an embrace, but in the bitter repudiation of a cross. If we allow representatives of the "new morality" to persuade us that "love is the only measure," we had better be clear and frank about whether the kind of love we are measuring with is that featured in the Gospel or in the novels of D. H. Lawrence; they are *not* the same.

The fact that extra-marital sex is often obviously selfish and irresponsible does not, however, excuse the cynicism of those who refuse to recognize that it can also be the expression of a very genuine mutual love, in which each of the lovers preserves a deep respect and even a primary concern for the values and needs of the other. Simply to damn such behavior in the phrase of earlier Catholic writers as "unlawful pursuit of venereal pleasure" can be most unfair to persons who really are more determined to give than to receive, and who fully appreciate the difference between showing love and seeking pleasure. When extra-marital intercourse is of this quality it can hardly be judged with harshness by anyone for whom love is the highest standard of moral evaluation. And one who merely concedes that subjective factors involved may save the situation from mortal sin is being grossly insensitive to real values and virtues. The claim that unmarried persons can have sexual intercourse with generous motives, clear consciences, and even real moral benefit is, I believe, supported by the testimony of too many good and perceptive people to be denied without arrogance.

Nevertheless, to admit and admire the real values that can be operative in extra-marital sex should not prevent us from asking whether, even at its best, there may still be something importantly wrong with it. I would conclude by suggesting that there is, but that it lies in a different direction from that of "unlawful venereal pleasure."

As the word implies, sexual intercourse is, among other things, an act of communication. When it is motivated by deep personal love, the physical act itself becomes suffused not only with feeling, but also, and much more importantly, with meaning. The core of that meaning has always been recognized as the mutual giving of oneself and acceptance of another. "Two in one flesh" is the physical symbol of a spiritual achievement which is the glory and dignity of sexual love. The essence of that achievement consists in the uniting of two human personalities by mutually assuming an unconditional responsibility for one another. This is the practical meaning of their mutual self-giving. But if this is the case, then the moral inadequacy of extra-marital sex results from the fact that the physical embrace says "I am yours" in a way that simply is not true unless the union has permanence and fidelity. In other words, I am maintaining that real lovers *know* that the kind of love their physical union expresses is one that promises not a momentary but a lasting union, and that the truth of their love must be tested by whether or not the future upholds its promise. When sexual intercourse embodies sufficient love to remove it from the realm of selfish, capricious pleasure-seeking, it becomes the best it is capable of being, and proclaims a gift of self. But if that gift turns out to have been merely a loan, then a radical insincerity lies at the heart of love's message. And with sexual intercourse, as with every kind of personal intercourse, one who brings himself to say more than he really means will find in the course of time that he has greatly weakened his capacity to mean as much as he says. I believe the greatest danger for the morality of those who practice outside of marriage a sexual love that is by no means mere lust is precisely this danger of becoming habitual liars in the language of love. The disastrous instability of marriage in our culture would seem to indicate that we have already gone very far in that direction.

Chapter 3

Respect for Life: The Abortion Controversy

During the past several years in America, "the abortion question" has referred to two distinct, although by no means unrelated questions. One of them has to do with the ethical status of abortion: Is abortion morally wrong? The other has to do with the legal status of abortion: Should abortion be against the law? One question, in other words, is about whether or not we should regard abortion as a sin, whereas the other is about whether or not we should treat it as a crime. Although our interest here is with morality rather than with law, in the case of abortion there are important moral aspects to the legal question itself, and the two cannot be completely separated.

The question about whether or not there should be laws against abortion became a major controversy in this country only during the past ten years. Previously, anti-abortion laws passed by various state legislatures were common, and their legitimacy and value seem to have been generally taken for granted. However, since the middle of the 1960's, a popular movement calling for the abolition of laws against abortion has grown rapidly in size and influence, and brought on a major social crusade through the popular media and the law courts. The outstanding victory of that crusade was achieved in January 1973, when the United States Supreme Court ruled that an anti-abortion law "that excepts from criminality only a life-saving procedure on behalf of the mother, without regard to pregnancy stage and without recognition of the other interests involved" is unconstitutional. The main practical effect of this decision is to leave the question of abortion previous to the end of the third month of pregnancy entirely up to the woman's physician. In later stages of pregnancy, laws still may not regulate abortion "where it is necessary, in appropriate medical judgment, for the preservation of the life or health of the mother."

During the years leading up to that historic decision, the movement in favor of legalized abortion drew popular attention to a number of factors that have greatly influenced opinion not only about the legal, but also about the moral question. The moral outlook of that movement itself is clearly expressed in the following statement by one of its leading spokesmen, Lawrence Lader: "What we were seeking, after all, seemed so profoundly just and humane. It was simply the right of personal decision, the right of a woman to control the creative powers of her body, to bring into the world only a child she truly wanted and loved. The use of contraception gave her this right to a considerable extent. But since many contraceptives had an inherent rate of error, or could fail, or were prescribed erroneously, or simply not used in a moment of abandon, contraception without the supporting right of abortion condemned women to biological chance. What we were seeking, further, could not infringe on the religious beliefs or political rights of any human being. . . . While any woman, no matter what her religion, could choose to end a pregnancy, neither a Catholic nor anyone else could be pressured into this choice."

Defenders of legalized abortion pointed out that anti-abortion laws had been created mainly for reasons which were no longer valid: to protect women from an operation which, before recent advances in surgical technology, was dangerous and unreliable. On the other hand, they pointed out that in recent times those same laws actually defeated their purpose, by compelling women to patronize incompetent and unscrupulous abortionists who either extorted exorbitant fees for flaunting the law, or neglected basic safeguards that would have been available in any legitimate clinic. It was also observed that whereas population growth was greatly desired at the time when anti-abortion laws came into being, that desire has since been replaced by fear of a population explosion.

The wording of the Supreme Court decision, together with the arguments of those who welcomed it as a victory, gives a fair idea of how the moral question of abortion presents itself to a great many Americans. In general, it is seen as a question of women's rights against a background of social problems. Anti-abortion laws are thought of as unjustifiable restrictions on the personal freedom of pregnant women. Abortion itself is seen as a potential safeguard of the life, health, or convenience of pregnant women, and at the same time as a contribution to easing social problems resulting from overpopulation and the birth of unwanted and defective offspring. In general, abortion is evaluated as a birth control measure, and justified on grounds similar to those applied to contraception. Abortion, like contraception, is considered a matter to be determined by private moral decision, although it is recognized to have important consequences for society as a whole. Moreover, entrusting abortion to the mother's decision on her doctor's advice is regarded as fair to all religious and ethical differences, since no one is obliged to act contrary to his own conscience or creed.

Throughout the whole crusade against anti-abortion laws, the most outstanding organized opposition came from the Catholic Church. That opposition was based on a view of abortion radically different from the one just described. Considerations of the mother's rights and of advantages to society were rarely referred to in Catholic statements, and the birth control argument carried little weight in view of the Church's rigorous doctrine on the use of contraceptives. Basic to the Catholic position was the question of the rights, not of the pregnant woman, but of what Catholics generally were careful to call "the unborn child," in contrast to their opponents who were equally careful to refer to it as "the fetal tissue." For Catholics, the abortion question has always been regarded primarily, and almost exclusively, as a question of the right to life.

One who talks about abortion as "removing some fetal tissue" obviously cannot feel quite the same way about it as one who calls it "killing an unborn child." Removing some tissue sounds like nothing worse than surgery, while killing a child sounds like nothing better than murder. In arguments between those who favor abortion and those who oppose it, each side tends to accuse the other of using a "loaded" vocabulary which appeals more to emotion than to reason. But while it is undoubtedly true that shallow sentimentality has played far too large a role on both sides of the abortion debate, the fact remains that the two expressions "fetal tissue" and "unborn child" clearly point to a crucial difference of opinion concerning a matter of fact which underlies this whole controversy. Unfortunately, about that question of fact there seems to be no present way, and perhaps not even any possible way, of achieving certainty.

To decide at what stage of the development that begins with a fertilized ovum the life of a real human person is actually present depends not only on biological information, but also on what one chooses to mean by a real human person. According to the Scholastic philosophy followed by most Catholic moral theologians, a human person is constituted by the infusion of a spiritual soul into an appropriate body—a theory which may be acceptable as metaphysics, but which certainly does not offer much help toward deciding concretely if an embryo at a given stage of development is or is not a human person. The often-cited opinion of St. Thomas, that the soul is infused forty days after the conception of a male and ninety days after the conception of a female, can scarcely be regarded as anything better than a guess, based on a very limited and largely erroneous knowledge of embryology. American law has traditionally assigned a different legal status to a fetus before the end of the twentieth week of pregnancy, inasmuch as a birth before that time is not classified as a delivery, and no birth or death certificate is required. The distinction made in the recent Supreme Court decision between the times before and after the end of the third month of pregnancy reflects the fact that the mother normally feels life within her womb near the end of the third month, and after that experience is likely to react to the fetus in a much more personal way. The fact remains, however, that the best information discoverable by embryologists points to no abrupt transition from sub-human to human life in the course of embryological development, but emphasizes the continuity of a development which is initiated and controlled by the genetic material received from the parents in the union of sperm and ovum. While striking differences are obviously apparent between different stages of pre-natal development, these are hardly more dramatic than differences which can be observed between infancy and adulthood.

In the present state of the evidence, to designate any stage of development before, at, or after birth as the true beginning of a human life can only be a rather arbitrary conjecture. For this reason, Catholic moral theologians have generally taken the position that since, to say the least, *any fetus may very well be* a *human being,* that possibility itself obliges us to respect its life in the same ways that other human life is respected. It is on this position that the Second Vatican Council based its strongly worded statement that "from the moment of its conception life must be guarded with the greatest care, while abortion and infanticide are unspeakable crimes" (*Gaudium et Spes,* 51). Given the facts of human development as they are currently known, it seems clear that to assume that any normally developing fetus is a piece of tissue representing something less than human life is intellectually irresponsible, and that to justify an action as drastic as abortion by such an assumption is morally irresponsible.

It is true, however, that schools of thought in modern philosophy and psychology have frequently identified "authentic personhood" with the exercise of individual freedom or the capacity for certain levels of social interaction. Since such criteria would disqualify from authentic personhood many adults who are in one way or another mentally, emotionally, or morally deficient, they have not generally been considered relevant to the abortion question.

Nevertheless, it is not at all unlikely that such criteria will be appealed to increasingly in the future. At least one influential Catholic writer has already adopted what he calls the "focus" of the "modern mind," which sees "no comparison between a fetus for which there is no sign of experience and a baby already in the process of experientially developing its unique personality and humanness in reaction to the persons around it." Even apart from the imprecision of the statement that a fetus shows "no sign of experience"—pre-natal behavioral responses have been extensively studied at remarkably early stages of fetal life—this "focus" of the "modern mind" seems a very blurred one, and in important respects more primitive than modern. It is really another example of our all too common tendency to limit what we think of as fellow human beings to those whose behavior most closely resembles and participates with our own. "People" thus comes to mean "people like us," and the unfamiliar becomes identified with the less than human. This attitude, currently used to justify abortion, has been used throughout man's history to justify a great many kinds of behavior that are now commonly deplored and condemned as "prejudiced" and "discriminatory." After all, it is not very long since basic personal rights were denied to blacks on the ground that they were obviously too unlike whites to be really altogether human. Perhaps an accusation that is too seldom heard by self-styled liberals who favor unrestricted abortion is that of flagrant discrimination based on rather crude prejudice. The morality of prejudice and discrimination will be the subject of a later chapter, but it is by no means unrelated to the question of popular attitudes toward fetal life. If the question of whether or not a fetus is human in the sense that a baby is human is at least a difficult and important question, what may be most significant in current controversy is not that pro-abortionists have their own answer to that question, but that they are so often unwilling to discuss it.

Granted that the principal moral question involved

in abortion is the right to life of an unborn child, it is
natural to look for guidelines in other areas where
moral theology must decide the rightness or
wrongness of taking human life. Until recently,
however, this has not generally been done. Instead,
a methodology has been applied to the question of
abortion which depends on a particular understanding of the principle of double effect, the result of
which is to forbid absolutely all direct abortion,
while allowing indirect abortion for a proportion-
ately good purpose. In applying this norm, however,
it is important to note that what makes an abortion
direct is understood to be the physical structure
of the act causing the death of a fetus, rather than
the intention of the person performing that act.
In other words, if a doctor uses an instrument
precisely to kill a fetus, or to remove one that
cannot survive outside the womb, according to
this theory it simply makes no difference why
he does it. Even in the extreme case where such
an abortion is used to save the life of a mother
who *could not survive otherwise,* by killing
a fetus which *could not survive anyway,* Catholic
moral theologians have generally taught that the
abortion, because direct, may not be performed.

I would suggest that we may need to review so rigid
a theory of direct abortion. I say this because hold-
ing this position leads to such fantastic consequences as in the hypothetical case just cited. Also
it is inconsistent with a more reasonable approach
which is actually taken in other situations. In order
to bring this out, let us compare the following two
statements, which occur on the same page of a

modern and reputedly liberal treatise of Catholic moral theology. (1) "It is not a sin to kill an insane man in order to ward off an attack on one's life or on the life of another, provided that the direct purpose of the killing is no more than a justifiable defense of one's own life or that of the third party, not the killing of the fanatical attacker, and that the defensive action does not exceed the actual requirements of self- defense." (2) "Even in the most extreme danger to the life of the mother, it is never allowed directly to cause or to intend a miscarriage."

Both of the cases just cited have to do with the killing of a human being (assassin or embryo). In both cases the killing may be regarded as direct (for example, a gunshot or surgery). In both cases the person who is killed is guiltless on account of his irrationality (insanity or immaturity). In both cases the motive of the killing is to save a life (victim's or mother's). The parallelism of the two cases is striking. Why, then, are the verdicts passed on the two cases diametrically opposite? Only, I believe, because of the narrowly physical interpretation of direct killing that has become associated with abortion. If, in the second case as in the first, we considered what is directly intended (the human motive) instead of what is directly done (the physical action), the result would be a justification of abortion, regardless of the technique used by the abortionist, on grounds of the proportionate good of saving the mother's life. I believe that by thinking along these lines, with an emphasis on motives, intentions, and the relative values of different consequences, we can arrive at a far more rational and humane approach to abortion than has usually been taken by Catholic moral theologians. However, in the present state of medical science, with adequate prenatal care such cases are so rare that they are largely hypothetical. Bringing a more open mind to solving the moral question involved in such cases does not in any way imply approval of the present almost indiscriminate abortions practiced in many of our states.

A final postscript might be added with regard to the very common opinion that the question of retaining or abolishing anti-abortion laws is a legal but not a moral question. If a citizen is convinced that a class of totally dependent human beings are in danger of grave abuse by those on whom they depend, it is ordinary civic morality to advocate laws which furnish suitable protection. It is on this basis that parental cruelty and neglect are subject to criminal sanctions. One who, regarding the fetus as an unborn child, is concerned to provide similar legal protection is reacting as a responsible citizen, not simply as a bigot or busybody.

Chapter 4

The Christian Family: The Domestic Church

As is well known, the Second Vatican Council, out of consideration for the Pope's wishes, avoided dealing with the issue of contraception. And although subsequent handling of that issue has not proved very satisfactory, in the eyes of some Catholics, the Council's treatment of marriage and the family in some respects undoubtedly gained by the omission. For the vehemence of controversy that accompanies Catholic discussions of birth control has had the unfortunate effect of causing that issue to overshadow other moral and theological aspects of Christian family life that are much more fundamentally important. By leaving it aside, however reluctantly, the Council was compelled to concentrate on other, more basic considerations. As a result, its account of Christian marriage and the family reflects a hierarchy of values which the contraception debate tends to obscure or distort. The present chapter will likewise leave the question of birth control to be treated separately, and briefly, at the end. Moreover, since previous chapters have dealt with sexuality generally and with abortion, and since subsequent ones will be devoted to questions concerning divorce and homosexuality, this chapter will also bypass those issues. It is the writer's conviction that one of the principal weaknesses of modern Catholic teaching on marriage and the family has been a grossly disproportionate preoccupation with the specifically sexual behavior of spouses. That there is a lot more (and better) to marriage than sex is undoubtedly a truism. But it is also a case for recalling G.K. Chesterton's reminder that "the important thing about a truism is that it is true."

A great deal of emphasis has been placed by contemporary theologians on the covenant relationship which Israel in the Old Testament and the early Church in the New regarded as the basis of both their union with God and their community solidarity. It has often been observed, moreover, that in the writings of the prophets, beginning with the book of Hosea, this covenant idea is translated into the striking imagery of a marriage between God and his people. The point of this marital symbolism was to emphasize that God's choice of his people was, like marriage, an act of love that expressed itself in commitment to unqualified fidelity and called for similar love, commitment, and fidelity in response. In other words, the prophets, assuming people knew that marriage basically entailed love, commitment, and fidelity, used it to explain that the covenant was based upon those same virtues. In the New Testament we find that not only is the same image applied to the relationship between Christ and his Church, but in one instance the force of its symbolism is even applied in the opposite direction. That is, whereas the Old Testament prophets used marriage to explain the nature of God's relationship with Israel, in the fifth chapter of Ephesians Christ's relationship with his Church is used to clarify the nature of the marriage.

In keeping with the recent emphasis on ecclesiology, Catholic writings on the theology of marriage have been strongly (though rather selectively) influenced by this passage from Ephesians. The same influence is expressed as a major theme in those portions of the Council documents which pertain to marriage. The following passage is typical. "The Christian family which springs from marriage as a reflection of the loving covenant uniting Christ with the Church, and as a participation in that covenant, will manifest to all men the Savior's living presence in the world and the genuine nature of the Church" (*Gaudium et Spes*, 48). Or, as the *Constitution on the Church* succinctly expresses it, "The family is, so to speak, the domestic Church" (*Lumen Gentium*, 11).

It may be recalled that for a long time there was heated controversy among Catholic theologians, which occasionally evoked strong words from the Vatican, over the so-called "primary and secondary ends of matrimony." The Second Vatican Council, however, avoided taking a side in this inconclusive debate. Moreover, in passages like the ones just referred to, the Council incidentally suggested a better way to answer the question of what marriage is for. For, as we read in the passage just quoted, what "springs from marriage" is, in the case of Christians, "the Christian family." And surely what marriage is for, what it commonly does, what it is normally meant to do is precisely to create that social entity which we call the family. Without marriage one can obviously have children, and may even do a fair job of raising them. Without marriage one can certainly have heterosexual companionship with or without any degree of mutual collaboration and erotic involvement. What cannot be had without marriage, or something so like marriage that to withhold the name is a mere technicality, is the thing we call a family. Love and cooperation between a man and a woman are not enough to make a family. Neither is sexual intercourse. Neither is bearing or rearing children. Families are complex realities which extend over all these things and more, while marriages are the relatively simple realities by which families are brought into being. I would suggest that if in place of contentious older answers to the question *de finibus matrimonii* we insert the more comprehensive term *familia*, our theology and ethics might have a starting point which corresponds more closely to the everyday experience of married people. It might also keep the thinking, especially clerical thinking, on this subject from being confined within the limits of bedroom and nursery.

My observation that marriage creates a family is one that other and older cultures would be quick to qualify, preferring to say that marriage continues or enlarges an already existing family. For it is distinctively modern and typically American to identify the family primarily or exclusively with a so-called "nuclear family" limited to parents and dependent children. It may be true that the broader, more clannish conceptions of family foster the development of values and perspectives which our culture is morally the worse for neglecting. Yet the social and economic forces which constrain modern societies to define the family more narrowly offer no prospect of being weakened or reversed in the foreseeable future. Indeed, what our "futurologists" generally envision is rather the final extinction of the family, with the absorption of its functions by other institutions. Given these conditions, the principal ethical dimensions of modern American family life correspond to the three orders of human relationships such families entail, namely, between the spouses, between the parents and children, and between the entire family and the rest of society.

Christian love is, of course, in a Christian family the moral norm for all human relationships. Nevertheless, in a family as in every society, the practical effectiveness of even such lofty motivation depends on a certain clarity and order which we associate more specifically with justice. Anciently defined as "a permanent and unwavering determination to give each one what he has a right to," justice is currently not a very fashionable virtue. However, the implication found in this definition of justice—that membership in any society entails definite rights and obligations—is something that the currently more fashionable virtue of love badly needs. The point is especially relevant at a time like the present, when Christian values are closely associated and often confused with those of Romanticism. For where considerations of justice are neglected in favor of unrestricted spontaneity in the expression of love, there invariably occurs an inconsistency of behavior which results, sooner or later, in confusion and strife. As we have already noted, our vocabulary of love is extremely ambiguous. So is much of the thinking it reflects. As a result, one can easily and sincerely invoke love as the motive and justification for actions that are morally inconsistent. This is probably one reason why children, despite all the talk about love that they hear, are much likelier to criticize the conduct of their elders and peers on grounds of fairness than on grounds of love. "It's not fair" is a much clearer complaint than "It's not loving," for it is based on the definiteness of acknowledged rights. And it is easy to observe that parents and teachers who seem thoroughly fair, even if not conspicuously loving, generally make young people a great deal happier, more productive, and more secure than do those who seem little concerned about fairness even though they may be very loving. An atmosphere of justice or fairness, where consciousness of basic rights and obligations is mutual and clear, is the only atmosphere in which Christian love can thrive constructively. For justice is to loving rather as logic is to thinking, a basis of order and direction which tests consistency and measures progress. Cultivation of justice, in the form of something like a code of fair play, is among the greatest needs of many modern families, where what begins in a harmony of spontaneous affection so often ends in a tyranny of whims and a turmoil of moods.

One reason this need is especially current is because of the rejection in recent times of earlier role prescriptions for the various positions in a family. In traditional households presided over by a "breadwinner" and a "housewife," the respective duties of husband and wife could in large measure be taken for granted. Moreover, they reflected a basic set of assumptions regarding the roles of the sexes generally. For many reasons, these traditional role expectations have lost much of their validity. What is expected of the various members of a family now depends largely on the family's own choice. Nevertheless, however roles and tasks are distributed, a family is no better able than other societies to function well without agreeing about them. Every society needs organization. In the past, the family's organization was mainly dictated by tradition. Now that it is not, the responsibility for organizing devolves upon the husband and wife. The failure of many to undertake such responsibility is the most decisive moral failure of many modern families. "If all were a single organ, where would the body be?" is an admonition initially made to the Church which is highly relevant to the contemporary "domestic church."

The obsolescence of traditional family roles affects the relationship between parents and children no less than that between husbands and wives. Urbanization and technology have gone far toward eliminating the usefulness of older children as helpers in family work, leaving these nearly-adult young people in the enervating and demoralizing roles of unconstructive dependents and unproductive consumers. Constant lengthening of the time given to formal schooling prolongs these roles and creates an artificially extended adolescence that sharply conflicts with normal physical and psychological development. At the same time, more and more of the educational functions that formerly belonged to parents are being relegated to a proliferating variety of institutions. The advantages in terms of technical efficiency and professional expertise are not unmixed blessings. Frequent revamping of institutions and their accessories constantly reduces the extent to which children's most vivid educational experiences correspond to those of their parents or even older brothers and sisters, thus contributing to the breakdown of understanding and communication within families. Moreover, the supposed ethical neutrality of secular education is altogether illusory. What specialists in moral education have been calling "the hidden curriculum," a set of implicit assumptions about human and social values, is invariably present and exerts an influence which is most effective where least perceived. The well-intentioned determination of many young couples to leave their children "free" to fashion their own ideals actually leaves them passive and vulnerable before a barrage of propaganda whose ethical implications are seldom admirable or consistent. Moral education within the Christian family has seldom been more needed, more difficult, or more neglected. The need of families for collaboration with competent people who share their values constitutes an urgent challenge to the intellectual and organizational resources of the Catholic Church.

In all moral education, actions speak louder than words. Far deeper ethical impressions are made on

children by what their families do than by what they
say. In this respect, however, what they do within
the family about one another is only a part of the
picture. The other part, what they as a family do
about those outside the domestic circle, is often an
area of moral blindness. For there is a deplorable
tendency in American family life to cultivate a kind
of isolationism that both our nation and our Church
have gone far toward discrediting and repudiating.
As a result, families frequently manifest collectively
a degree of selfishness and insensitivity which few
of their members would succumb to individually.
All too often, a marriage of idealistic young people
proves fatal to broad social sympathies, generous
self-sacrifice, and the healthy asceticism of normal
adaptation, endurance, and risk, while opening the
way to seemingly insatiable demands for comfort
and security. The selfishness of such a way of life,
disguised by the fact that all the superfluities are
amassed for "one another," has been well characterized by the phrase *égoisme à deux*, two-party
egotism. Whether or not charity begins at home, if it
is Christian charity it does not remain there. What
has already been said of the Church's need to be ec-
umenical in its sympathies and apostolic in its ener-
gies applies, for identical reasons, to the spirit of
hospitality and service that must characterize the
"domestic church."

I have deliberately posponed treatment of the birth
control question until after discussing some broad
moral aspects of family life that seem especially important in contemporary circumstances. In doing so,
I have frankly wished to imply that the consciences

of Christian couples (and of those who advise them) have more important matters to deal with than contraception. Moreover, I am confident that couples who are not conscientiously concerned about the matters we have been considering will both give a selfish answer to the question of how to regulate the size of their families, and never for a moment suspect that there is anything selfish about it. In any case, it is only the couples themselves who can answer that question conscientiously, in the light of their own capacities and needs, and those of their actual and prospective children and of the community at large. All that can be done by others is to remind them of their responsibility for weighing those factors, help them do so on the basis of correct information, and advise them about practical and acceptable means to implement family planning.

In the latter connection, Catholics notoriously find themselves in an embarrassing position. The most recent papal encyclical on the subject, issued five years ago, condemns certain popular chemical and mechanical methods of contraception as contrary to natural law. At the same time, the professional opinion of a majority of theologians, philosophers, physicians, and social scientists, including those selected by the Pope himself to advise him, fails to support the encyclical's conclusion. Similar disagreement is found among the clergy, while on the part of the laity it finds expression in open disregard. Under such circumstances it is scarcely possible to speak unambiguously of "Catholic doctrine" on the means of birth control. It is possible to describe "papal doctrine" on the question. And the distinction is especially important because the Pope's doctrine is presented not as an account of Christian revelation, but as an interpretation of natural law, that is, of principles of morality supposedly discoverable by man's natural reason. Since, however, the natural reason of a majority of acknowledged experts fails to arrive at the same conclusion as that expressed in the encyclical, the correspondence of that conclusion with natural law necessarily remains questionable. Under such circumstances, it is the duty of whoever confronts the practical issues of birth control to inform himself as accurately as he can with regard both to the facts and to the principles involved, and then—after thought and prayer—to make his decision on the basis of all of these factors. My own position with regard to such principles has been outlined in the chapter on sexual morality.

Chapter 5

What God Has Joined

There can be few social institutions on which Christianity has made a deeper or more unique impression than the institution of marriage. In a number of respects, Christianity's attitude toward marriage contrasts as strongly with that of Israel as with those of ancient paganisms and modern secularism.

But there can be little doubt that the most distinctive feature of Christian matrimonial tradition has been, from the very earliest times, its insistence on the permanence of the marriage bond. Moreover, it is on this point exclusively that we find evidence of a doctrine explicitly enunciated by Jesus Christ. The relevant biblical data entail problems of interpretation which we cannot dispose of here. But a review of the principal texts is indispensable to a theological evaluation of current attitudes and proposals concerning divorce.

The oldest New Testament document which touches on the matter is St. Paul's first letter to the Corinthians (7:10-16). Here St. Paul distinguishes between two points of doctrine, the content of which we shall examine later. The source of the first, Paul says, is "not I, but the Lord," whereas the source of the second is "I, not the Lord." Therefore, Paul and presumably many of his readers were familiar with a teaching by Christ himself on the indissolubility of marriage. And as he describes that teaching, we easily recognize it as the doctrine attributed to Jesus by each of the three Synoptic Gospels, recorded by one passage in Mark, one in Luke, and two in Matthew. There are significant differences of context and wording among these passages. But what they have in common is so clear and consistent, and in such perfect accord with what St. Paul recalls as the Lord's own teaching, that it is reasonable to assume that, as far as it goes, it represents the teaching of Christ himself. The substance of that teaching is a condemnation of divorce as contrary to the will of God, with the implication that remarriage by divorcees is equivalent to adultery. Granting that much, however, account must be taken of important differences among these passages.

The passage in Mark (10:1-12) is introduced by a question asked of Jesus by the Pharisees concerning the legitimacy of divorce. Since we are told it was designed to "test him," they apparently had reason to believe Jesus would find it an embarrassing question, to which he would have to give an unpopular answer. The Pharisees were expounders and defenders of the Mosaic law, and every Jew knew that Mosaic law permitted a husband to divorce his wife (but not vice versa), though opinions differed about what grounds were required to justify his doing so. Jesus accordingly replies by asking what Moses commanded, and is told that Moses directed them to divorce by giving a "writ of separation" (a merciful provision for the rejected wife, freeing her to remarry). Conceding this, Jesus nevertheless goes on to interpret the Mosaic provision as a concession to "hard-heartedness." He then appeals beyond it to the creation account in Genesis as expressing what is truly God's will, namely that those who marry become "one flesh." And against this background Jesus' doctrine is succinctly expressed in the famous pronouncement, "What God has joined together let man not take apart."

Mark's Gospel pursues the question a further step by having the disciples reopen it "back in the house." Jesus is there made to amplify his statement by declaring that either a husband who divorces his wife or a wife who divorces her husband commits adultery by remarrying. This would seem to imply that the original marriage actually remains in force. The reference to a wife's divorcing her husband describes a possibility under Roman, although not under Jewish law.

In Luke's Gospel (16:18) the episodes involving Jesus' dialogue with the Pharisees and the disciples are not recorded. Instead, within a long series of disconnected sayings we find Jesus' statement that one who divorces his wife and remarries commits adultery. But in place of Mark's parallel indictment of the wife who divorces her husband, Luke adds that one who marries a divorced woman commits adultery, thus remaining within a perspective that is both Jewish and legalistic.

In Matthew's Gospel two separate passages pertain

to our comparison. The longer of them (19:3-9), despite differences in wording and in the order of phrases, is for the most part same as Mark's account of Jesus' exchange with the Pharisees. However, Matthew includes within this context, and in a significantly altered form, the teaching which in Mark was addressed separately to the disciples. A minor discrepancy is that Matthew, like Luke, does not refer to the case of a woman who divorces and remarries. A much more striking difference is that adultery is here charged to the man who divorces his wife "except in a case of unchastity." This notable exception likewise appears in an abbreviated version of the passage which is contained in the Sermon on the Mount (5:31-32). Despite centuries of theological and philological discussion, both the meaning here of the word rendered as "unchastity" (*porneia*, which normally means fornication), and the explanation of why Matthew alone contains this "exceptive" passage remain uncertain. It is known that in Christ's time the strictest school of rabbinical interpretation limited the Mosaic concession of divorce to the case of a husband whose wife was guilty of adultery (which *porneia* here might possibly mean).

Returning at last to the teaching of St. Paul from which we began, first of all we find it there presented as the Lord's doctrine that a wife may not leave her husband and remarry, nor may a husband divorce his wife. But Paul proceeds to offer a further opinion of his own having to do with the situation of Christians married to pagans. If the pagan spouse is willing to continue in such a marriage, Paul says the

Christian should not divorce. But if the pagan decides to separate, that should be permitted, in which case the Christian spouse is no longer bound. Paul's regretful and reluctant attitude toward even the divorce he does allow is emphatic throughout this whole passage, which ends with an exhortation to see in the preservation of marriage with a pagan spouse an opportunity to fulfill the Christian vocation: "God's call is a call to live in peace."

So brief a summary of what we find in the New Testament concerning divorce obviously cannot deal in any detail with the texts or various interpretations of them. Nevertheless, consideration of the passages we have described, in the light of accepted principles of biblical exegesis, readily establishes two points, both of which need to be borne in mind. One is that the condemnation of divorce is a very ancient and very emphatic element of Christian tradition, and one which there are excellent grounds for ascribing to an explicit teaching of Jesus Christ himself. It appears to have been based on the understanding of marriage as designed by God to constitute a virtually organic union between the spouses. The second point is that from a very early date in the history of Christianity, exceptions to the absolute proscription of divorce were admitted, apparently in both Jewish and Gentile Christian communities. In the case of Matthew's Gospel, the exception seems to have been derived from conservative rabbinical teaching, whereas in Paul's case it was based on his personal assessment of a contemporary social dilemma.

Admittedly, the text in Matthew is complicated by the fact that the exception is presented, if not very convincingly in the light of other New Testament references, as part of Christ's own statement. But leaving that question undecided, the Pauline text makes it perfectly clear that exceptions to the exclusion of divorce were by no means unthinkable in the apostolic Church. In view of the rather mystical aura with which Canon Law has surrounded the so-called "Pauline privilege," it needs to be emphasized that Paul himself is deliberately unpretentious about the source of his doctrine. It is "I, not the Lord." In other words, without minimizing Paul's apostolic authority, we should note that he clearly avoids making any claim that his position is guaranteed by public or private revelation. Thus, even though Paul shows himself fully aware of Christ's rejection of divorce, he does not hesitate to advocate it as a last resort when a pagan is unwilling to remain with a Christian spouse.

Before exploring this matter further, let us introduce a contemporary question that may guide us in doing so. Could the pastoral authority of today's Church act in a manner similar to St. Paul with respect to marriages between Christians that lie outside the "Pauline privilege?" The spontaneous conservative reply will presumably be negative, on the familiar grounds that such marriages, being sacramental, fall unexceptionably under Christ's law of indissolubility. But before accepting such an answer several considerations should be raised. A relatively minor one is that although consummation is not held to be a condition of sacramentality, unconsummated Christian marriages have long been regarded as capable of dissolution. Another is that, as nearly as we can reconstruct the context of Christ's words, they certainly did not refer to what canon lawyers mean by a sacramental marriage; they referred either to marriage in general (as the appeal to Genesis suggests), or precisely to Jewish marriage (as the Pharisees and disciples would have expected). But most important of all is the idea, strongly emphasized in modern biblical theology, that passages like those on divorce are gravely misapprehended when they are conceived as legal enactments on the part of Christ, although evidence of such misapprehension is found within the New Testament itself. The fact that Christ's saying on divorce is inserted within the Sermon on the Mount may serve to remind us that it ought no more to be regarded as a law than other statements contained there concerning Christian behavior. In the same chapter of Matthew where Christ forbids divorce he also forbids oath-taking and retaliation. Yet, while canonists have regarded the prohibition of divorce as a law, they have not developed a similar view of the other two prohibitions. Nor, we might add, does Christ seem to be taken quite so seriously when he imputes adultery for lustful looks as when he does so for second marriages!

These sayings of Christ are not flights of rhetoric. But neither are they enactments of law. For the centrally important fact is that Christ simply was not a law-maker. It has been well said that his statements about human conduct are "not law but Gospel."

That is, they are not legislation, they are revelation. And what is revealed is not some prototype of the *Codex Iuris Canonici*. It is the kingdom of God. These statements are representative of the kind of living that characterizes the kingdom of God. But that kingdom, inaugurated by Christ's redemptive death and resurrection, is not yet wholly in possession of this world. Rather it is locked in combat with powers of darkness whose overthrow, though assured, is not completed. Yet nowhere does Christ condescend to explain how we are to "get along" with this grace-resisting, God-repudiating world by adjusting our plans to the consequences of its unregenerate behavior. And yet we are obliged to do so, and to figure out for ourselves how to do so. That is why, for instance, one who responds in faith to Christ's words against violence can yet never hope to extract from the Gospel a "socially practical program" of non-resistance. Christ tells us what it is like to live the life he offers us, the life of the kingdom, the life of love, the life of God. And that this is something very different from law is among the most insistent messages of New Testament theology.

Christ's saying on divorce, unlike most of his other sayings about human conduct, has been treated as a law. St. Paul, who has been the Church's greatest teacher in this matter, knew better. He saw clearly that to keep one's marriage intact was the Christian thing to do. But he also saw that in certain circumstances the Christian thing could not be done. And he accordingly recommended making the best of an admittedly bad thing. "God's call is a call to live in peace." But if somebody can't, because somebody else won't, then let us do the best we can. Christ's rejection of divorce and his accusation of adultery are simply other expressions of his insistence on what marriage is supposed to be: two in one flesh, a living union wrought by love in conformity with the creative wisdom of God. If the reality of that union is shattered, regardless of what legal formalities do or do not accompany its shattering, God's wisdom is stultified, his creation is spoiled, the damage is done, the divorce, if we allow that term any but juridical meaning, is already a fact.

That is what Paul saw as already inevitable once a pagan was determined to be rid of his Christian spouse. Paul did not, in that new-born Church of Corinth, entertain the possibility of a similar issue's being prevalent in marriages between Christians. But now, of course, in our own churches, it is. And in such cases, with or without legal divorce, the thing Christ proclaimed before the Pharisees as his Father's will, the two in one flesh, is already dismembered. And when that happens, life, however diminished, must go on for the Christian as best it can. Under those circumstances, good laws are those human arrangements which help it to do so.

A reform of our marriage laws is increasingly called for. To do the job adequately will require the immense task of purging the Church's canonical tradition of a great many erroneous or doubtful theological assumptions. It will necessitate a clear distinction between Christ's revelation which is wholly the work of God, and the Church's legislation which, though not unassisted, is wholly the

work of men. There are no revealed canons. There is
no canonical revelation. Christ's revelation certainly
appears to tell us something about marriage. It tells
us what God created marriage to be and what,
therefore, it is meant to be in the life of the kingdom
of God. The Church's legislation must be primarily
concerned to help marriages be what Christ tells us
marriage is. But if a marriage, by fault or impersonal
circumstance, is irreparably prevented from being
what it is meant to be, it would seem wise for the
Church to follow the example of St. Paul. In St.
Paul's church the "unbelievers" could be identified
with the unbaptized. But in our own churches there
is many a marriage between a Christian and an "un-
believer" both of whom are baptized. And between
them situations often arise like those that concerned
St. Paul in Corinth. Nothing prevents our following
St. Paul's example in behalf of the authentic Christians in such marriages except a decidedly questionable doctrine about the baptism of the spouses making their marriage sacramental and consequently
indissoluble. It is time that the evidence in support
of that doctrine was conscientiously evaluated in the
light of unprejudiced historical and theological research. Until that is done, we have no right to be
surprised, much less indignant, if the consciences of
certain individuals find themselves sincerely at
variance with the implications and demands of existing law.

The last reflection suggests an issue related to the
question of divorce which has recently been much
discussed. It has to do with the exclusion from the Holy
Eucharist of persons officially regarded as involved

in "bad marriages." The crucial case here is that of one who in the light of his own conscience is reconciled with God even though that fact is not, and perhaps cannot be legally demonstrated, a case of irremediable discrepancy between the "internal" and "external" forum. A minister of the Eucharist in such a case is faced with a conflict of testimony. The course of action he follows would presumably be influenced by the following considerations. First, Canon Law itself acknowledges that no excommunication can be valid unless the cause for which it is incurred entails grave subjective guilt. Second, no one but God and the supposedly excommunicated individual can possibly know, except by the latter's testimony, whether or not that condition is fulfilled. Third, one who refuses the Eucharist to such a person does so on the basis of a juridical presumption concerning something which the law, admittedly, does not know. Fourth, one who allows the Eucharist to such a person does so on the basis of personal trust concerning something which the individual, if anyone, does know. The choice then, is between transmitting Christ's gift in response to a personal assurance of innocence and need, and refusing it in response to an impersonal presumption of guilt and unworthiness. For a minister of the Gospel of forgiveness and love, is not the right choice, under such circumstances, fairly obvious? And should not the law, preaching, and habitual practice of the Church encourage him to make that choice?

Chapter 6

The Persistence of Samaritans

I can only guess what memories linger most indelibly in the minds of most theologians who have traveled in Palestine, but I doubt if my own experience is typical. For I find that neither the scenes of Jerusalem, Bethlehem, and the Galilean lakeshore, nor any of the remarkable sites of biblical archaeology return quite so readily and vividly to my imagination as does one nondescript little town where I spent only a portion of one day. Nablus, as the town is called, is a place on which neither nature nor art has bestowed beauty. It is a place of undisguised poverty, lassitude, and dereliction. It is a place whose unhappy blend of isolation and insufficiency is epitomized in the signs, frequent among its population, of an unwholesome physiognomy symptomatic of prolonged inbreeding. This rather pathetic community of a few hundred persons, a tiny theocracy whose prized possession and main tourist attraction is a twelfth century manuscript of the Torah, is what remains of the people called Samaritans.

It is, of course, both highly ironic and deeply significant that in European languages generally, the noun

Samaritan has been so commonly preceded by the adjective good, that the phrase itself, good Samaritan, has long been included in our dictionaries. The fact is significant as indicating the influence on Western culture of the parable of Jesus preserved in the tenth chapter of the Gospel according to Luke. And it is ironic as representing a complete reversal of the traditional associations with the word Samaritan that the parable takes for granted and from which it derives its principal moral force. It is as though the cowardly lion in *The Wizard of Oz* had made timidity the trait we chiefly associate with the king of beasts; or as though *Ferdinand* had conditioned us to think of bulls as characteristically languid and sentimental creatures. When the phrase "good Samaritan" loses the force of paradox, the parable itself loses much of its meaning.

For in the lifetime of Jesus, Samaritans had long been regarded by Jews as a wholly contemptible people. The seeds of this animosity had been planted five centuries before, when Persian clemency made it possible for exiled Israelites to reestablish themselves in their ancestral homeland. On their return they found the territory called Samaria inhabited by a population of mixed ancestry, including both Israelites who had never been sent into exile and Mesopotamian colonists who replaced the deportees. Although this mixture had introduced religious diversity, the worship of Yahweh seems to have prevailed, and when returning Israelites undertook the rebuilding of the temple the Samaritans were eager to join them in this historic task. They were, however, harshly rebuffed and treated as an alien and undesirable people. With understandable resentment, the Samaritans sought afterward to sabotage as enemies the work they were prevented from sharing as friends. Their opposition ultimately failed, but the mutual animosity it had kindled proved inextinguishable. Samaritan separatism found expression in their construction of a rival temple on Mount Gerizim, and theological reinforcement in their heretical refusal to admit the canonicity of any biblical writings outside the Pentateuch. From accidental circumstances of history, to discrimination, to exclusion, to feud, to schism, to heresy—deterioration of their relationship with the Samaritans had by Jesus' time produced in the Jews an inveterate bitterness that expressed itself in institutionalized patterns of ostracism and contempt. By then, the Samaritans were immemorially an outcaste people, and how they had become so no longer made much practical difference. That their very name had degenerated into a term of obloquy is apparent in the words addressed to Jesus by his enemies in John's Gospel: "Are we not right in saying that you are a Samaritan and that you are possessed?" (Jn. 8:48)

It was, of course, precisely because of what Samaritans had come to represent for Jews that Jesus chose a Samaritan for the moral hero of his story. A similar determination to put Samaritans in a shockingly favorable light appears elsewhere in the Gospels, as where Jesus rebukes his disciples for wishing to invoke God's punishment on Samaria (Lk. 9.52), where the only one of ten lepers who thanks Jesus for his cure is identified as a Samaritan (Lk. 17:16), and where the Samaritan woman at the well is made an exemplar of faith (Jn. 4). But it is the parable of the man who fell among robbers that most effectively exploits the attitude of the Jews toward the Samaritans and, in the process, most effectively discredits it.

The parable derives its meaning from the fact that it is Jesus' answer to the question, "Who is my neighbor?" and that the question was asked with a view to specifying the implications of the twofold commandment of love. Jesus' choice of a priest and a levite to represent the practical denial of love brings into sharpest possible relief the contrasting behavior of the Samaritan. One could scarcely contrive a more vivid way to emphasize the irrelevance of restricted social categories to the perspective of Christian love. The very structure of the parable compels the hearer to bring together two ideas habitually assumed to be irreconcilable, the idea of neighbor and the idea of Samaritan.

But the structure of the parable also does something else. For on first reading or hearing it one may very well have an uneasy feeling that the *status quaestionis* has subtly shifted between the question and its response. For the question was "Who is my neighbor?" which the context makes equivalent to "Whom must I love in order to gain eternal life?" No direct answer is ever given to this question. Instead, against the narrative background supplied by the parable, Jesus responds to his questioner by asking in turn, "Which of these three do you think *was neighbor* to the man who fell into the hands of the robbers?" Is this the question one logically expects him to ask? Does it come to terms with the question that was put to him? Ought he not rather to have asked, "Which of these three *perceived as his neighbor* the man who fell into the hands of the robbers?" The original question was about identifying the neighbor as *one who is to be loved*. But Jesus' question identifies the neighbor as *one who does love*. No doubt, the word neighbor implies mutuality. Being a neighbor means being someone's neighbor, which further implies recognizing that someone as one's own neighbor. All this is indisputably true, but it does not change the fact that Jesus' question introduces a significant difference of viewpoint. For his questioner, neighbor has a mainly passive connotation; the point is *whom* to love. But for Jesus himself, the connotation of neighbor is primarily active; the point is *how* to love.

Accordingly, the parable of the good Samaritan does not conclude by providing any criterion for determining who is entitled to one's love. Instead, its concluding words are, "Go and do as he did." What did he (the Samaritan) do? He loved. How did he love? Compassionately, unselfishly, actively, effectively. Whom did he love? From one point of view, a fellow human being in obvious and immediate need of help. From another point of view, an anonymous representative of an alien, arrogant, offensive, oppressive majority. The shift of viewpoint which the parable introduces is one which compels us to think of the neighbor rather as the active bestower than as the passive recipient of love. And implicit in this alteration of viewpoint is the definite refusal of something Jesus' questioner had obviously been looking for. "Who is my neighbor" was only another way of asking "Who is not my neighbor?" What the questioner was seeking was a basis for discrimination between neighbors and non-neighbors. No such basis is provided by Jesus' teaching because no such discrimination is admitted by it. If anyone might be expected and entitled to discriminate between neighbors and non-neighbors, it would seem to be a Samaritan with respect to Jews; for Jews had been discriminating between Samaritans and neighbors for five centuries. And so, to a Jew who wishes to discriminate Jesus tells the story of a Samaritan who refuses to discriminate and says "Go and do as he did."

Refusal to provide a basis for discrimination between neighbors and non-neighbors, between those whom we must and those whom we need not love is profoundly characteristic of the Christian's morality as it is profoundly characteristic of the Christian's understanding of God as revealed in and by Jesus Christ. The only discrimination appropriate to Christian love is discrimination of the need for it. Accordingly, in the Gospel it is where the need for love is most acute that the insistence on love is most emphatic. We see this above all in the pattern of Christ's love, which is so conspicuously preferential in its treatment of those whose need for love is greatest. Moreover, the same pattern incessantly reminds us that needing love has little to do with what is normally meant by deserving love. Thus it is the sinner who most needs God's love, though it is also the sinner who least deserves it. And so it is the sin-

ner whom the Gospel most emphatically assures of
God's love. The meaning of the incarnation has
often been expressed by the saying that God became man so that men might become as God. That
formulation of Christian faith is also the formulation
of Christian ethics, the whole essence of Christian
morality. It is revolutionary in its prescription for
human love only because and to the extent that it is
revolutionary in its description of divine love. The
revolution in faith and the revolution in morals are
one and the same. But a revolution it surely is.

In the long history of Christian exegesis of the parable of the Good Samaritan one finds, especially in
former centuries when allegorical interpretation
generally prevailed, a preoccupation with es-
tablishing whom the Samaritan in the story "stands
for." For some he "stands for" the good Christian.
For others he "stands for" Christ. For still others he
"stands for" God the Father. But it was also
frequently observed that here we do not really have
strictly alternative interpretations. For all of these
participate in a single continuous pattern of divine
love in which each implies and expresses the others.
What that pattern is, and what the Christian revolution in faith and morals is, has its most famous summary in the Sermon on the Mount, in a passage
which is perhaps the best and clearest of all commentaries on the parable of the Good Samaritan:

"You have learned that they were told, 'Love your
neighbor, hate your enemy.' But what I tell you is
this: Love your enemies and pray for your persecu-
tors; only so can you be children of your heavenly

Father, who makes his sun rise on good and bad alike, and sends the rain on the honest and the dishonest. If you love only those who love you, what reward can you expect? Surely the tax-gatherers do as much as that. And if you greet only your brothers, what is there extraordinary about that? Even the heathen do as much. There must be no limit to your goodness, as your heavenly Father's goodness knows no bounds" (Mt. 5.43-48). This is the answer to "Who is my neighbor?" This is the meaning of "Go and do as he did." This is Christian faith and this is Christian morals; and they are one. This is the meaning of the Gospel and this is the message of the Church; and they are one—or are they?

Merest honesty compels us to admit that the kind of discriminatory love which violates the basic meaning of the Gospel has to a shocking degree survived and even flourished in the Church which professes to live by and for that Gospel. For many individuals, discrimination of the harshest kind between neighbors and non-neighbors, insiders and outsiders, "us" and "them" seems to be the most conspicuous and compelling feature of Church membership. And the Church collectively has exposed its preaching to charges of blatant hypocrisy by its notorious habit of disintegrating, on the slightest provocation, into bitterly and even violently hostile factions. For most people, even rather ruthless people, no hatred seems quite so despicable as *odium theologicum*. I remember wondering, as I entered the famous Museum of Atheism and Comparative Religion which occupies what was once a great cathedral in Moscow, what one could possibly exhibit in such a place with a view to demonstrating the non-existence of God. What I expected were exhibits of scientific and technological achievements which, by exalting the triumphs of rationalism and materialism, mocked the naïveté of religious faith. Some of that was present, but what I remember most clearly were exhibits of a quite different and probably much more effective kind: exhibits of the virulence and violence of Christian history, with all its "religious" persecutions, "sacred" inquisitions, and "holy" wars, a pageant of Christian hypocrisy. The atheists had taken the Christians at their word, had met them on their own terms, had condemned them out of their own mouths. See how they love one another! "A city set on a mountain cannot be hid!" Sometimes one wishes that it could!

In our own time, unfair discrimination—racial, ethnic, religious, sexual—and its sources in bigotry and prejudice have become matters of unprecedentedly widespread and popular concern. It has been extensively studied in an effort to determine the relevant social and psychological factors as a prerequisite for designing effective programs aimed at reform. Inevitably in the course of this research data were collected and analyzed with a view to exploring the relationship that actually exists between prejudice and religion. Superficially, at least, these findings have been most disheartening to any but opponents of religion. For religion, and in particular Christian religion, far from appearing to discourage discrimination and prejudice, shows every indication of complacently harboring and even of actively fostering them. On balance, the best that researchers have been able to say in this respect for religions in general, or for the Christian churches taken either collectively or singly, can be summed up in the following statement by an outstanding student of the question who is himself a convinced and practicing Christian: "It is clear . . . that religion bears no univocal relationship to prejudice. Its influence is important, but it works in contradictory directions. The apologists for religion overlook its ethnocentric and self-exalting reference; its opponents see little else."

There are also, however, in the social research we have been alluding to, other findings which religious people, and especially religious leaders, should find helpful and constructive if by no means flattering. For it is clear that where prejudice and discrimination find fertility in religious soil, that soil is of a distinctive kind. In general, it is where religion has become identified, popularly if not officially, with cultural and ethnic rather than spiritual and transcendental values, that it fosters discrimination and prejudice. It is where worship emphasizes ostentatious ritual or smug sociability at the expense of the simplicity of contemplation and the humility of adoration. It is where fashionable viewpoints and local preoccupations displace the essence of the Gospel as the focus of preaching and discussion. It is where the triviality of churchmanship replaces the seriousness of discipleship. It is where the crudity of legalism replaces the delicacy of conscience. It is where the shallow complexity of the words of men replace the profound simplicity of the Word of God. What can religion do about discrimination and prejudice? Only as much as religion can do about itself. Nothing could be plainer than that there is no room in the Gospel of Jesus Christ for discrimination and prejudice. And if there is such ample room for them in our churches it is only because there is so little room in our churches for the Gospel of Jesus Christ. To cope with these matters the Church does not need new programs or modern policies. It desperately needs the old program, the original policy. It does not need to broaden its field. It needs to sharpen its point. The point of its "two-edged sword," without which the Church is, in any sense of the word, pointless.

Meanwhile the Samaritans are still there—in Nablus —still here—in America—still everywhere. But so is the word Jesus spoke to a Samaritan woman. "The time approaches, indeed it is already here, when those who are real worshippers will worship the Father in spirit and in truth. Such are the worshippers whom the Father wants. God is spirit, and those who worship him must worship in spirit and in truth" (Jn. 4.23-25).

Chapter 7

Drugs: The Choice and the Alternatives

Drugs, of whatever kind, are for their users primarily a means of escape. Apart from yielding to curiosity or social pressure, one considers taking drugs because the physical or mental state in which one finds oneself is more or less unsatisfactory and one has reason to hope that drugs may improve matters. It is, at least initially, a matter of choice, and there are alternatives. One can, for example, simply put up with the unsatisfactory state, usually with some hope that it will eventually improve without direct intervention. Or else one may try to improve the situation by means other than drugs. And finally, if one does decide on drugs there still remains a wide range of choice among those which are relatively safe and relatively dangerous, cheap and expensive, legal and illegal. The "drug problem" which looms so large and dark on our present social horizon consists basically in the fact that more and more people are more and more frequently choosing drugs over any alternative means for coping with unsatisfactory conditions of mind and body, and that the drugs chosen are often dangerous, expensive, and illegal ones. Moreover, when it comes to analyzing this problem in any greater detail, and still more to prescribing means to solve it, there is widespread disagreement about both the facts involved and the values at stake. Although our own concern will be chiefly with the latter, the frequency of unsupported statements and inconsistent findings about drugs and their users which can be cited from medical and legal literature on this problem makes it more than usually necessary to be very wary of prejudice and very insistent on evidence.

One important observation which was generally absent from earlier discussions of the drug problem has recently become widely recognized. And that is that the widespread recourse to drugs which especially characterizes our youth can scarcely be regarded as an original and radical departure from the cultural example set by their elders. On the contrary, the present younger generation are less the creators than they are the inheritors of a "drug culture." Americans have long been characterized by something approaching a popular mania for habitually seeking the solutions to all sorts of problems in bottles, capsules, tablets, and syringes. That a generation of youth who grew up among elders, so many of whom seemed incapable of achieving sociability without alcohol, serenity without tranquilizers, alertness without stimulants, relaxation without sedatives, or endurance without analgesics, should have pursued their own real or fancied happiness by pharmacological means is scarcely remarkable. Nor, by the same token, is there anything remarkable in the fact that shocked self-righteousness on the part of elders about their off-spring's use of drugs is commonly resented by the latter as hypocrisy. I vividly recall the irony of one particular father whose preparation for the painful duty of discussing his son's reported use of pot consisted in fortifying himself with gin to the point of almost total incoherence.

In this respect, the American drug problem is only a particular manifestation of the much larger and much more complicated problem of American reliance on technological means to achieve ends that were formerly sought by ethical and spiritual ones. It would be interesting to explore in detail the extent to which such goals as mastering recalcitrant moods and adjusting to critical circumstances that were formerly the objects of a character formation based on abstinence and austerity have in our own time become the objects of habitual dependence on a chemical technology that fosters consumption and indulgence. One writer who recalled a conversation in which an American LSD devotee equated his own conveniently obtainable ecstasy with what an Indian guru achieved through prolonged self-discipline and meditation has suggested that it was not unlike a dialogue between one man who had scaled the Matterhorn and another who had been set on top of it by a helicopter. One who climbs a mountain gains considerably more than a view from its summit—and retains it considerably longer.

One of the major difficulties of coping with the drug problem is undoubtedly popular ignorance. Unfortunately, however, the kind of ignorance that prevails is one of the hardest kinds to overcome. For it is based not on a simple absence or sparsity of popular information on the subject, but rather on an enormous excess of popular information that is biased, disorganized, and incomplete. The facts about drugs are presented to the general public mainly by the popular press and by intensely partisan advocates or opponents of the use of drugs. And the fact that these sources are so available as to be practically unavoidable, and that a veritable deluge of information constantly flows from them has the deplorable effect of preventing most people from acknowledging, or even suspecting, any need for better information. Better information is, of course, available, but it is very seldom sought and very little known by non-professionals. Among these must be included the average clergyman, teacher, parent, policeman, politician, and voter, all of whom have decidedly important roles to play in dealing with the drug problem.

The average American, I should guess, thinks of the drug problem mainly in terms of pot, heroin, and LSD. He thinks of it as mainly a youth and ghetto phenomenon. He associates it with cultural eccentricity, incidental violence, and organized crime. He regards it as a situation that is bad and growing worse. He suspects that marijuana may not be terribly dangerous in itself, but supposes it commonly leads to things that are. He links heroin mainly with crime and LSD mainly with madness. He looks for a solution mainly from the medical and legal professions, and sees the solution in terms mainly of rehabilitation and deterrence. That is, his recommendation for the drug problem is, in general, better clinics and better laws, more clinics and tougher laws, the former to help people get out of drug trouble and the latter to keep them from getting into it.

In the preceding sketch of what I suggest is the popular impression of our current drug problem, one significant feature is the identification of the drugs themselves. The drugs that are on everyone's lips are marijuana, heroin, and LSD. The reason why they are on everyone's lips is because they are so widely publicized in the popular media, and because much of the publicity they receive is of a highly sensational character. An attempt has frequently been made to point out the most outstanding omission from the average man's mental list of problem drugs. But despite such attempts, and despite the fact that the omission is a glaringly obvious one, popular thinking continues to be largely uninfluenced by reminders that the drug most widely used by Americans, and the one which causes by far the most extensive damage to their physical, mental, social, and moral lives, is, unquestionably, alcohol.

A couple of years ago the *New York Times* ran an advertisement paid for by Blue Cross, under the heading, "The Biggest Drug Problem in America Is Right There in Your Glass." The rest of the ad was devoted to justifying that statement by pointing out that the chemical nature of alcohol and the physiological effects of its consumption clearly indicate that it belongs to the general category of what are called drugs, and that the statistics of its involvement in the causation of death, physical and mental disability, and social crisis are of a magnitude that dwarfs all comparable statistics for all other drugs, even collectively. The advertisement certainly attracted notice and elicited vigorous reactions. Of the reactions it did elicit, however, those which received maximum publicity were highly indignant ones by, of all people, public relations executives of major manufacturers of alcoholic beverages. Despite such doubtfully objective assurances, it is a fact that according to the best evidence available on a much-studied subject, something like one out of every ten drinkers in this country goes on to alcoholism. Moreover, the present number of known alcoholics in the U.S. is not less than nine million, and may be as many as twelve million. Not only, therefore, is alcohol by far the most widely used drug, but it has also by far the highest rate of disabling effects.

Second only to alcohol in popularity is marijuana, and if its use continues to increase at the present rate, it will not be very many years before it wins first place. Since its popularity in our culture is relatively new, and characteristic of the younger generation, it remains to be seen whether, as that generation grows older, its use will spread uniformly among all age groups. At any rate, for the five years between 1967 and 1972, affirmative answers to the Gallup poll question "Have you ever tried marijuana?" rose from less than five to more than fifty percent of the people asked. Although its use has already become too common for identification with any sub-culture, its popularity is greatest in the middle class, and among those otherwise inclined to rebelliousness and social non-conformity. In significant contrast to the figures for alcoholism, comparable disability seems to result from use of marijuana in fewer than one percent of cases. Under such circumstances, it is impossible not to sympathize with the resentment of marijuana users to legal sanctions and social stigmas that are imposed on them but not on users of alcohol as discriminatory, irrational, and hypocritical. The likelihood of solving any social or moral problem with laws that are vulnerable to such criticisms is, to say the least, not very great. And, given the close association in our culture between the use of marijuana and anti-establishment feelings, it should be obvious that such a legal policy is bound to be not only unhelpful, but self-defeating. One of the major moral issues related to the drug problem is precisely that of the justice of our present laws. Another, closely related to it, is the shocking disproportion between public support given to enforcing anti-drug laws and that given to providing and maintaining therapeutic facilities. Such figures as those recently publicized for the state of California, showing public funds for anti-drug law enforcement to be fully ten times what is spent on all resources for therapy, should inspire moral indignation and political protest in any conscientious citizen.

The exaggerated public reaction to marijuana, and its paradoxical contrast with public complacency concerning alcohol, suggests some of the more critical weaknesses in our handling of the drug problem. First, there is an emphasis on police control and penal sanctions which borders on fanaticism, and which is proving as ineffectual in dealing with the drug problem as it has been with a number of other social problems of recent years. Second, there is a habitual failure to recognize in practice that the threats posed by different kinds of drugs vary enormously both in kind and in degree. Third, just as very little attention is given to the implications of what specific drug is being used, so, too, very little effort is made to determine the difference between use and abuse. In the latter connection, a recent book by a medical authority on drug therapy offers the following plausible definition: "Drug abuse: the presence of demonstrable psychological or social dysfunction in any individual which can be causally related to the use of a drug, either acutely or chronically." What is astonishing and appalling is the observation the writer appends to that definition, that "to date, in the Western World, no such definition or approach has been used to understand drug abuse." As long as our public policies are so compulsively oriented toward getting drug offenders into courtrooms and jails that they employ no sensitive criteria for determining the nature or evaluating the seriousness of their "offenses," neither justice nor efficiency is likely to prevail. Nor is it encouraging that our federal government's narrow "law and order" approach to the drug problem was finally somewhat broadened in response not to medical or ethical opinion, nor to the tragic conditions of urban poverty and indignity that have driven so many to addiction, but to the embarrassment of widespread narcotic addiction among veterans returning from Vietnam.

Few of those who use drugs, and fewer still of those

who use them excessively, do so naively. The dangers of heavy indulgence in alcohol have been well advertised for a very long time, during which alcohol consumption, and alcoholism, have continued to increase. The dangers of cigarette smoking have been documented to the satisfaction of the most skeptical, but cigarette manufacturers are doing a pretty good business. Since warnings about the danger of marijuana and psychedelics are widely suspected of gross exaggeration, their deterrent force is negligible. The destructive capacity of amphetamines and barbiturates is commonly known, but their use, and medical prescriptions for their use, become ever more frequent and ever more casual. And the constantly depicted horrors of narcotic addiction appear to have no more inhibiting effect than the prices extorted by hustlers or the penalties inflicted by law. Why do they do it?

A good many experienced investigators who have asked that question of drug abusers report having received the reply "Why not?" or "Show me something better." To such responses many a "straight" reader is inclined to retort that "it's obvious why not" or that "anything would be better." The common ground of such disagreements is the important recognition that the use and abuse of drugs is, after all, motivated behavior. It represents a choice. The choice is made in the face of alternatives, and expresses the rejection of available alternatives. A number of investigators have also asked many who have given up their formerly habitual and abusive use of drugs why, or how, they stopped. Rarely do their replies express simply a fear of the damaging consequences of drug consumption. Usually, the reason given is much more positive, involving the discovery of some value or goal, irreconcilable with the drug habit, which makes giving up drugs worthwhile. "Show me something better" may be said flippantly or cynically, but the words express the very heart of the matter.

We said at the outset that drugs are for their users primarily means of escape. And the moral issue of drug use is, therefore, for the individual user, in part the morality of escapism. To some, it would seem that escapism is by its very nature immoral, so that to recognize drugs as escape mechanisms is sufficient for their moral condemnation. But surely such a position cannot be seriously defended. There is nothing inherently wrong or right about escaping; it all depends on what you are escaping from and what you are escaping to. And there are clearly plenty of drug users who have no doubt at all that what their use of drugs gets them into is decidedly preferable to what it gets them out of. As long as such a point of view claims many adherents, the drug problem will certainly not be solved. And at present, for not a few of our fellow citizens, that point of view seems inescapable. The physical and social environment in which they are compelled to live is such that escapism presents itself as the only motive, one might almost say the only ideology, that really makes sense. And all too often the only escape that lies open to such people is through drugs. Many a doctor regularly prescribes continued use of drugs to relieve a degree of anxiety and pain that is mild by comparison with that which drives less fortunate

sufferers to a use of drugs for which they are pun-
ished as criminals.

I have no wish to imply that drug abuse is morally
blameless, though morally blaming it is hardly likely
to improve matters for anyone. Unquestionably it is
frequently self-destructive, and simultaneously destructive of other persons and even of whole communities. Undoubtedly drugs are often adopted to
escape, not from an intolerably oppressive environment, but from the basic vicissitudes, responsi-
bilities, and tasks whose acceptance is the very making of a man. But often too, such escapes are
achieved by perfectly legal means, while penalties
of law fall most heavily on the harmless, the help-
less, and the hurt.

Chapter 8

Honesty: A Name for Many Virtues

Honesty, and its opposite, dishonesty, are among the most frequently used words in our moral vocabulary when we talk about morality in non-technical language. Generally one would not find them in the index of a book of moral theology or a treatise on philosophical ethics. One reason for this is because, as our use of the word honesty has developed, it has no precise equivalent in other languages. What an American means when he speaks of an honest man is something quite different from the classical *vir honestus*, as well as from such modern derivatives as *honrade* or *onesto*.

In Latin, and languages closer akin to it than ours, these words remain closely associated in meaning with their background idea of "honor." As a result, what is uppermost in their connotation is the notion of being honored or respected. They express qualities for which we might employ such words as propriety, decency, or respectability. It is a peculiarly English development of language that honesty has come to refer not to the social or public acceptability of a person or his behavior, but to an intrinsic moral quality, or perhaps a number of such qualities. For a vivid if trivial illustration of the contrast, one might recall that "dishonest parts" would scarcely convey in English the idea of those portions of the human body whose presumed unfitness for unveiling in public led to their being called "partes inhonestae!"

It is easier to say, however, what honesty does not mean in English than what it does mean. A few examples may suggest its range of meaning. A clerk who habitually short-changes customers certainly qualifies as dishonest. So does a manufacturer who grossly misrepresents the quality of his product. So does a man who poses as a doctor without having studied medicine, or any impostor who takes advantage of people's misplaced confidence. Burglary is considered dishonest. So is graft. So is cheating, in a game, in an academic examination, or in a political election campaign, where cheating is understood to mean violating the rules publicly agreed upon to assure fair competition. Similarly, breaking public laws seems to be called dishonesty only when it has the quality of cheating, that is, when it is the means by which some people take unfair advantage of others.

If we reflect on these and other examples that come readily to mind of what would normally be labeled dishonesty, I think we shall find that most if not all of them fall within two traditional categories of immorality, namely, untruthfulness and injustice. By the same token, what we call honesty can usually be described as truthfulness or justice. Just how distinct these are is a further question, which can be answered more confidently after they have first been considered separately.

Truthfulness, in theory if not in practice, has fair claim to being the most popular, meaning the most admired and commended, of moral virtues in our contemporary American society. In any case, it is talked about incessantly, and often with considerable passion. An illustration of this fact is the overuse of the modern phrase "credibility gap," which has long since made it a foremost American cliché. The popularity of this phrase reflects the high degree of public sensitivity not only to the prevalence of liars among us, but to the effect their lying has had in destroying the degree of mutual confidence and trust that is vital to the health and happiness of society.

We live in a culture in which consciousness of rampant deceit has generated a pervasive atmosphere of skepticism and cynicism. With some, reaction takes the form of habitual insistence on positive proof, with minimal regard for the value of mere personal assurances. Such phrases as "You can take my word for it" or "I give you my word of honor" have become, as perhaps never before, powerless to convince. To stake one's honor on the truth of one's word is widely regarded as too cheap a guarantee to be taken seriously.

Ironically, the very witnesses whose reputation for truthfulness has suffered most scandalously in our time compound their offensiveness by their insistence on using the most arrogantly impersonal means for avoiding deception. This is most conspicuous on the part of government, which on the one hand has earned an appallingly general reputation for insincerity, and on the other hand has placed unprecedented reliance on insidious techniques of spying that are contemptuous of the most elementary rights of privacy. As official assurances grow ever more widely discredited, official intelligence relies ever more heavily on bugging, wire-taps, and other refinements of espionage. One detects an ominously plausible pattern: that just as trustworthiness and trust tend to thrive together, so too the readiness to deceive and the dread of being deceived go hand in hand. It is the most uninhibited liars who make the most uninhibited spies.

It is noteworthy that the "credibility gap" is very frequently linked with the other most talked about of our society's ethical gaps, the "generation gap." Remarkably often, the categorical complaints of the young about their elders are a concentrated indictment of the latter's insincerity, hypocrisy, or "phoniness." "Telling lies to the young is wrong" is the opening line of a poem that never fails to win the sympathy of campus audiences during American college tours by its Russian author.

Many of those who might be called our social "elders" or authority figures—for example, government in the eyes of so many citizens, and parents in the eyes of so many children—find themselves popularly situated on the far side of a credibility gap. Even teachers and ministers, whose vocations have often been described in terms of dedicated service of the truth, are increasingly stigmatized as self-seeking propagandists and obscurantists.

Even among many of those who clamor most loudly for truth, especially under the title of "personal authenticity," one cannot but be impressed by the widespread disregard for and even disparagement of what in the past has been widely regarded as morally the most important kind of truthfulness. And we are thereby reminded that to talk about truthfulness as a virtue requires making some basic distinctions. For example, the kind of truthfulness which has in recent years been most admired and cultivated, especially among the young, is that which we characterize more specifically as "candor," "frankness," or "openness." It refers to the habit, or policy, or practice of saying what one "really thinks" or expressing what one "really feels," and is therefore opposed not only to falsifying one's thoughts or feelings, but also to concealing them, which in many cultures is, at least occasionally, thought of as virtuous.

On the other hand, in the traditional morality of our own culture, truthfulness as a virtue has demanded not only that one's words be true to one's thoughts, but also, and perhaps more insistently, that one's deeds be true to one's words. That is, truthfulness or truth was regarded as a matter not only, or even mainly, of self-expression, but of self-commitment. It is in this latter sense that one is said to be "true" to his promises, or to his principles, or to his vocation. It is in this sense that the verse, "Ah love, let us be true to one another," means something quite different from "Let us be perfectly frank with one another."

To recognize the difference between these two senses of truth as a moral and personal attribute leads to the further recognition that they can, in fact, come into conflict with one another. For the more closely we identify truth as a virtue of candid self-expression, the more likely we are to see it threatened by truth in the other sense of adherence to commitment. Whereas the former emphasizes spontaneity, what the latter stresses is steadfastness. And it not infrequently happens that steadfastness can only be effectively maintained at the expense of spontaneity. Accordingly, for example, a man may, in abandoning his wife for another woman, be most true to his feelings by the very behavior which makes him most untrue to his promises. On the other hand, to remain true to his promises, he might find it necessary, at least for a time, to conceal his thoughts and dissimulate his feelings. It is in the way such conflicts are resolved that one discovers which sort of truth ranks higher on a person's scale of values. In our day an abundance both of words and of deeds suggests increasing preference for the former and ever-diminishing esteem for the latter.

Since our perspective here is a theological one, perhaps the most appropriate observation to make about this prevailing cultural attitude toward truth is that the kind of truth which seems today to be more in honor, whatever its merits, finds little to recommend it in distinctively Christian moral tradition.

The candor, openness, or uninhibited self-expression which is currently so much extolled in religious circles has little or no connection with the mainstream of Christian ethics from earliest to most recent times. Its historic patron is not Christianity but Romanticism. On the other hand, the other notion of truth as a virtue can lay claim to the strongest support in biblical and theological tradition.

It is this latter sense of truth which is represented as a virtue of God himself. The truth of God is precisely his steadfastness, his resolute adherence to his promises. It is on this truth that the covenant is based, and with it the hope of salvation. And it is in virtue of this truth that man responds to and participates in the covenant; it is the very meaning of our Amen.

One might be helped in comparing these two kinds of truth by reflecting on the celebrated example of St. Thomas More, whose heroic effort to remain true both to God and to country compelled him for so long to conceal his most pressing thoughts and dissimulate his most intense feelings, to sacrifice spontaneity, frankness, and openness to a steadfast adherence to both his Christian and his civil commitments. It is a case that brings out an important aspect of this whole matter: that whereas truth in the sense of fidelity to valid commitments, the image of God's own truth, is intrinsically virtuous, truth in the other sense, of openness or candor, sometimes certainly is, but sometimes definitely is not, especially admirable behavior.

We have said that the examples of honesty which do not fall easily under the heading of truth or truthfulness would seem to be instances of what is normally called justice. But in fact, if we think of justice as the respecting of rights, as giving people what they have a right to, it would seem also to include truth in the sense of adherence to commitments. For the very fact of making a promise involves bestowing on someone the right to have that promise kept. To give one's word is to assume the obligation of keeping one's word, and to keep one's word is merely to act justly toward those to whom it has been given.

The other aspect of what we usually mean by honesty pertains to the commonest understanding of justice, mainly in the sense of fairness in exchange (commutative justice), and fairness in sharing (distributive justice). In neither of these fundamental areas of social morality has there been any remarkable modern development in Christian ethical thinking, but there are certain characteristically modern points of view that may be worth reflecting on. One of these is the recurrent tendency to identify Christian moral ideals with something like a socialist economic ideology. It is not my purpose here to criticize, much less refute, socialism, with which, in fact, I have very strong sympathies. I wish rather to call attention to what seems to me a misguided tendency in what some Christians conceive as the application of theology to social thinking and planning.

Put very simply, it comes to something like this.

Christian morality, with its primary emphasis on universal fraternal love, logically places great stress on giving to and sharing with others. This giving and sharing extends to virtually everything we can dispose of in our lives, but it is most palpably applicable to our material possessions. Material generosity, made possible by a character liberated from the acquisitiveness and tenacity of greed, is certainly an essential and conspicuous aspect of a personality refashioned in the image of Christ. Nevertheless, this Christian generosity simply cannot, as some appear to imagine, be directly and logically translated into the ideology of socialism. The reason why it cannot may appear most clearly from two points of view.

To illustrate the first, we may take a classic Gospel exemplification of the kind of generosity Christianity advocates and examine it from a socialist moral perspective. The example I refer to is the episode recounted in the Gospel of Mark (12:41-44; also Lk. 21:1-4), where Jesus called attention to a poor widow whose "mite" he described as being a greater offering than all the lavish contributions of the rich, because "those others who have given had more than enough, but she, with less than enough, has given all she had to live on." Such a commentary on such an occurrence makes sense from a Christian point of view—but from no other! Consequently, it does not make the slightest sense from a conscientiously socialist point of view. On exclusively socialist ethical principles the widow had no reason—one might even argue convincingly that she had no real right—to give as she did. Her circumstances were

such as entitled her to receive, and obliged those in
more comfortable circumstances to give to her of
their own superfluity. She was, if you care to put it
that way, clearly entitled to "welfare." Given socialist politics, her right to receive and their obligation
to provide would be respectively protected and enforced by law, but the right and wrong of such a
case is clear enough regardless of politics and independently of law.

Now although it is beyond doubt that Jesus would
have readily admitted, and even insisted upon, the
widow's right to be provided for in her need by
those who could easily do so, that was not the point
he chose to make. Social justice of this kind was a
constant theme of the prophets that is clearly
echoed in the New Testament. Nevertheless, as
Jesus presented it, the widow's poverty signified not
her ordinary right to receive, out of bare justice, but
her extraordinary opportunity to give, out of pure
love! Moreover, this same point of view is entirely
characteristic of Jesus who, without by any means
rejecting the morality of social justice which had for
centuries been eloquently expressed in Israel, neither emphasized nor developed it in his own teaching.

What he did emphasize was a love whose generosity
transcends the domain of justice even to the point
of scandalizing the domain of reason—as does, in its
small way, the story of the widow and, in its great
way, the "folly" of the cross. The point is not that
Jesus was opposed to or indifferent to social justice,
or even a socialist way of achieving it. The point is

that Jesus was typically, and essentially, talking about something quite different. The moral perspective of the Sermon on the Mount was no more designed to reform political economy than the faith that moves mountains was designed to replace bulldozers. If everyone lived the Sermon on the Mount, political economy would be made, not perfect, but utterly irrelevant. But as long as we continue to pray "thy kingdom come," that point has not been reached, and in the meanwhile we must do the best we can about things like political economy. And in doing the best we can about such things, we who are Christians will find in the Gospel motivation and inspiration, but we shall not find—and we should only do harm by pretending to find—detailed instructions.

The other point of view to which I referred earlier is one that brings out the inappropriateness of Jesus' teaching to social and political revolutionary purposes. For whereas revolutions characteristically depend on some group of "have-nots" forcibly taking something (whether rights, or powers, or riches) of which they have been deprived, forcible taking, however justified it may be in given circumstances, is, once again, simply not part of what the Gospel is talking about.

"Take it, you have a perfect right" unquestionably may, at certain times, be excellent advice and wholly consonant with justice. But does Jesus in the Gospels ever say anything remotely like that to the deprived or underprivileged? Again, that is not what the Gospel is about. And one of the reasons why

Christians so frequently lose sight of what the Gospel is about is because of their insistence that it must be about such things as these. Jesus did not come to teach us to be decently honest and basically just. But unless we are, or are trying to be, it is very unlikely that we shall ever learn what he did come to teach us.

Chapter 9

Perverted, Queer, or Gay?

For a trustworthy compendium of what was long accepted as sound Catholic sexual morality, one can scarcely do better than to review the relevant section of St. Thomas Aquinas' *Summa Theologiae*. Within that section, his discussion of sexual vices occupies Question 154 of the *Secunda Secundae*. And within that Question, his discussion of "vice against nature" is contained in the 11th Article, which distinguishes four varieties of such vice, and the 12th Article which argues that these constitute collectively the worst kind of lust, but also establishes among them a scale of relative badness. The first category is masturbation, the second bestiality, the third sodomy, and the fourth, for which neither Latin nor English seems to offer a simple label, is "failure to observe the natural way of intercourse."

When these are rearranged in descending order of wickedness, bestiality stands at the top of the list, followed first by sodomy, and then by failure to observe the natural way of intercourse, with masturbation occupying the lowest (that is, least bad) position. Although the philosophical niceties of this doctrine were never officially endorsed, acceptance of both a general condemnation of these kinds of behavior, and of a need (in confession, for example) to distinguish among them, is stated or clearly implied in several papal pronouncements, mainly from the 17th and 20th centuries.

And yet, I think it is safe to say that very few—even of the most conservative Catholics in our own time —would regard as either heretics or libertines those who find much of this doctrine highly questionable or even plainly wrong. And I imagine the widest agreement among such critics would be found with regard to the idea that the kinds of behavior just described represent the morally worst that man's sexual conduct is capable of.

If we reflect on the views and values of modern Catholics, which prevent them from regarding "unnatural vice" as the most sinful kind of sexual behavior, we shall find that what is common to them all is a basic strong conviction about the primacy of love (*caritas, agape*) as the sovereign standard for all of Christian ethics. And since this conviction is more plainly insisted upon by Jesus in the Gospels and throughout the rest of the New Testament than anything else in the whole realm of morality, one can scarcely call such an approach disreputable. But once that approach is adopted, certain conclusions seem to follow at once.

Imagine, for example, the morally worst you can in the categories of the "unnatural vices." And then perform the same feat of morbid imagination for the "natural vices." And then compare. Can we really bring ourselves to place even the worst conceivable sodomists, bestialists, or masturbators farther from the kingdom of heaven than the worst conceivable rapists, adulterers, and seducers? And is not the reason we find it so hard to do so because the latter examples are so much richer in capabilities for thwarting, despising, and destroying love? Are not, in fact, those "natural" kinds of behavior in which our sexuality can most perfectly express love, the very same ones by which we can most grievously betray it? Is it not with "healthy" sex, as with healthy bodies generally, that man can do his morally worst as well as best?

However, unless we are so smug as to suppose the theological superiority of our own age to all earlier ones—a really ludicrous claim as soon as one even glances at the evidence—at least one rather humble question ought to occur to us. What about Thomas Aquinas—to say nothing of the illustrious predecessors and followers who agreed with him? Did he really get to be a saint without having paid as much attention to the importance of Christian love as the dullest hack writers and trite preachers of modern piety seem to have done? And did he really qualify as a doctor of the universal Church without having suspected that the primacy of love might have some applicability to sexual morality?

Rhetorical questions though these may be, we are not limited to our own common sense presumptions in answering them. For if we turn once again to the *Summa*'s contention that the worst sins of lust are those of unnatural vices, we shall find the modern love-centered repudiation of that position clearly enunciated in the very first objection with which Thomas confronts his thesis. It would be hard to phrase it more pointedly: "Any sin is the more serious the more contrary it is to love. But adultery, the rape of a young girl and sexual abduction, which inflict unjust harm on one's neighbor, seem more contrary to love than unnatural sins by which nobody else is injured. Consequently unnatural sin is not the worst kind of lust."

The fact that Thomas raises this objection so clearly makes it evident that at the very least he understands such a way of thinking. And the further fact that he does not dispose of it by simply denying the principle that "sin is the more serious the more contrary it is to love" would be inexplicable if he did not, in fact, take for granted the supposedly modern idea that love is normative in sexual morality. And indeed, to anyone who troubles to read Thomas, contemporary assertions of the primacy of love in Christian ethics seem little better than inarticulate echoings of his own constant, cogent, and emphatic teaching.

Although I strongly share the modern view that Thomas was mistaken in attributing greater sinful potentiality to "unnatural" than to "natural" sexual behavior, we should realize that he did not reach that conclusion by arguing against the primacy of love, but by arguing from it. But where modern talk about the "twofold law of love" seems to draw moral conclusions only from the second part of that law, Thomas took the "first and greatest commandment" seriously. When he condemned "unnatural vice" as strongly as he did, it was because it appeared to him to be contrary to the love of God himself, an abuse of God's gifts and contravention of God's creative and providential plan. And for Thomas, that meant responding to the very essence and source of love with nothing short of contempt.

If we feel justified in departing from the tradition Thomas represents, it is not because we know more than he did about Christian love or Christian theology; most of us know infinitely less about both. It is rather because we both know more and assume less than he did about nature. Not theological acumen but scientific and technological developments have taught us that nature—every nature and all of nature—is enormously more complicated than Thomas ever dreamed. We have found so much that looked like regularity, stability, simplicity, and uniformity to be merely a superficial impression of what deeper scrutiny reveals as randomness, agitation, multiplicity, and variety. In a culture deeply impressed by such discoveries in every field of empirical learning, the idea of the "natural" becomes too naïve or too arrogant a conception, and in practical matters less and less usable. A philosophy based on neatly definable natures preserves its internal coherence at the expense of its applicability to the world of experience.

I remember an academic discussion of homosexuality toward the end of which one participant tried to get it back onto familiar ground by proclaiming that "nevertheless, homosexuality is unnatural!" To which someone else impatiently but not unwisely replied: "Homosexuality is perfectly natural—to the homosexual!" Apart from being clever repartee, such an answer bears an interpretation that is both true and important. For in good popular usage, any pattern of reaction that appears native, spontaneous, insistent, potentially satisfying, and unextinguished by the ordinary experiences of life, is surely what we call natural.

If such a pattern of reaction is very different from the usual, and therefore hard to harmonize with the firm expectations of society and the institutions built on those expectations, we speak nowadays not of the unnatural but of the abnormal or deviant. When the abnormal is perceived mainly as uncomfortable for its subject, a benign and resourceful society may seek to alleviate it or, failing in that, to make discreet allowances. When it is seen rather as menacing to society itself, stronger efforts are made to conceal, confine, or expel it. In our society, homosexuals have experienced both kinds of treatment; in the past mostly the latter kind, and at present increasingly the former.

The first major transition in society's perception of the homosexual may be reflected in the substitution of "queer" for "pervert" in a popular vocabulary of disapproval. In any case, perversity has a significantly different meaning from queerness. Whatever is perverted is initially and basically oriented in one direction, but then violently turned or twisted some other way. This probably comes close to the thinking of St. Thomas, who refers not to homosexuality which is itself a deeply rooted sexual orientation, but to sodomy, which he conceives as an irrational and violent displacement of the natural tenor of all sexuality.

The general acceptance of homosexuality as an unavoidable complication in our very notion of sex is one of those steps toward a truer but less tidy understanding of the world. And once we start thinking in terms of a "queer" variety of person, called homosexual, instead of a "perverted" kind of activity called "sodomy," the whole point of view represented by St. Thomas in this matter becomes largely irrelevant.

By adopting an alternative point of view, we are led to recognize "sodomitic" behavior as, in a perfectly defensible sense, "natural—to the homosexual." For we now see the homosexual not as one who *is* different because he *acts* differently, but who *acts* differently because in one respect he *is* different. For the homosexual, no less than for the heterosexual, "*agere sequitur esse.*" Most of us, and indeed most homosexuals, will undoubtedly agree that the way a homosexual *is* constitutes a difference which has to be called a defect. But even granting that, from such a point of view it might seem hardly more perverse for a homosexual to seek erotic gratification from his or her own sex than for one born or made mute to "talk" with his hands, or for a deaf person to "listen" with his eyes. For all of these situations, one may desire and seek a "cure" which, in most cases, would be very gratefully received, but failing that, it is obviously necessary to think in terms of making "the best of a bad thing." The deaf mute could, of course, simply do without any kind of conversational gratification, but few of us would want him to do so or admire him for doing so. The homosexual could, likewise, simply do without any kind of erotic gratification. Are we justified in wanting him or her to do so? Or in morally condemning or legally penalizing him or her for doing so?

The last of these questions is the easiest to answer. Legal penalties exist to protect the community against injury. To the extent, then, that homosexual practices threaten the community with injuries that only criminal sanctions are sufficient to deter, laws against them should undoubtedly be enacted and enforced. But I doubt that such laws would need to be very different from those that properly restrict heterosexual practices. Children, for example, should undoubtedly be protected from homosexual abuse. But should they be any less protected from heterosexual offenders? And is obscenity less morally objectionable when its themes are heterosexual than when they are homosexual?

The law should, I think, exercise over sexual behavior a surveillance that requires a degree of self-control which spares innocent and defenseless persons from violence and corruption, intervening only where that degree of responsibility is lacking. For legal intervention to go farther than that is both unjust, because exceeding the purpose of criminal law, and ineffectual, because unenforceable without intolerable violations of privacy. Criminal law is an instrument not of individual sanctification but of community protection. That instrumentality is no more wisely served by penalizing the homosexual practices of consenting adults than by prosecuting adults for "garden variety" fornication. And the same should only be said more emphatically of that unofficial kind of pulic prosecution which is undertaken so eagerly in our society by self-righteous purveyors of scandal.

From any standpoint based on Christian values, it would seem that the most serious moral problems related to homosexuality are to be discovered not in how homosexuals behave, but in how heterosexuals have behaved toward them. It is notorious that our sexually "normal" majority have habitually, with varying degrees of subtlety, taken it upon themselves to punish homosexuals merely for being what, usually for no fault or preference of their own, they are. This ugly punitive frame of mind is manifested over a whole spectrum of characteristic overreactions, ranging from cruel jokes to cruel laws. It reflects a psychology of its own which is vastly more unwholesome and dangerous than the deviant tendencies it attacks, betraying that ruthless kind of defensiveness which is usually attributable to insecurity and fear. Probably it is one of the many symptoms of that anxiety about sexual adequacy and identity which is among the sickest characteristics of our culture. It is also one of many sad illustrations of the psychology which underlies all forms of irrational prejudice, bigotry, and intolerance. It is inconceivable that any intelligent and conscientious Christian should believe that society is more imperiled or God more offended by homosexuality than by, say, pride, greed, envy, or infidelity. And yet our society which not only tolerates, but deliberately glamorizes and systematically rewards these latter vices, reserves for homosexuality the full impact of its moral indignation. We have not yet ceased to "strain for the gnat and swallow the camel!"

Having been so long condemned to jail and to hell as "perverts," or to ridicule and ostracism as "queers," it is no wonder that some homosexuals should attempt to fashion a compensatory culture of their own. Whatever pretensions it may make to some kind of esoteric superiority, the "gay" world is all too visibly a sad world. Like homosexual lovemaking itself, it represents an effort to make the best of a bad thing, to make a ghetto a fashionable neighborhood, an exile a desirable resort. There is something pitiable about the posturings one so often observes in "gay lib" circles as they present themselves to an unsympathetic "outside world." But there is also something admirable in the resistance of the human spirit to accepting classification as socially contemptible.

In referring to homosexual practices as efforts to "make the best of a bad thing," and in comparing the abnormality of their behavior to compensatory techniques developed by others kinds of handicapped persons, I did not meant to beg the question of their moral justifiability. But I think the comparison has definite bearing on a sound moral evaluation. Homosexuality is no simple entity. It ranges from that occasional erotic responsiveness between persons of the same sex which is perfectly ordinary and, by every indication I know, perfectly healthy and normal, to an extreme condition which excludes every kind of heterosexual activation, while leaving homosexual outlets the only ones available for any kind of sexual satisfaction. With regard to cases of the latter kind, moral judgment must seriously confront the stark alternative: homosexual practices or total celibacy. Total celibacy is not a synonym for total disaster. It has a highly respectable status in the Christian scheme of things— as a way of life freely undertaken for the highest of motives. Jesus in the Gospel narrative describes it as "something which not everyone can accept, but only those for whom God has appointed it." And he concludes: "Let those accept it who can" (Mt. 19:12).

But are we quite certain that "God has appointed it" for all homosexuals? And is there some implicit guarantee that "those who can accept it" includes all homosexuals? Has total celibacy an equally honorable place in the Christian scheme of things as a way of life to which certain persons for whom it is acutely painful are permanently consigned? And which they are expected to embrace from no higher motives than the assumption that heterosexual incapacity excludes all but sinful alternatives? On the basis of those standards of sexual morality which were proposed in an earlier chapter, I do not see how such a position can be defended as certain or imposed as obligatory.

Chapter 10

Societies as Sinners

Only a person can sin, because only a person can love. For it is only the ability to love which makes it possible to refuse or reject love. And that alone is what Christians mean by sinning. For to sin is to disobey those commandments—to love God and to love our neighbor—on which "the whole law and the prophets" depends. It is necessary to keep this in mind from the outset of any discussion about what is called "social sin," because it sets important limits to the acceptable meaning of that phrase. Above all, it warns us against understanding social sin as referring to sins or kinds of sin which are, strictly speaking, committed by societies rather than by individual persons.

I do not, of course, mean to deny that societies, as distinct from individual persons, can do a great deal of harm. Still less do I mean to deny that the harm they do is often attributable to sin. When we speak with moral indignation about "unfortunate victims of society," we are realistically recognizing the existence of such harm, as well as of the sinfulness which causes it. But to speak of a society as a sinner is always either a metaphor or a misunderstanding.

And there is probably some danger that the popularity of the metaphor contributes to the frequency of the misunderstanding. That is doubly unfortunate, because the metaphor, when free of misunderstanding, expresses a valuable insight.

Rather than pursue this question further in the abstract, let us consider a concrete example of what can certainly be called social sin. The example I propose has the advantage of being unusually simple and clear-cut. The society in question is conveniently small, and it is exclusively Christian, being more or less what we would think of as a parish. And the sin in question is by Christian standards unmistakable, being equally a failure in love both of God and of the neighbor. The situation is described as follows, by St. Paul, commenting on the liturgical behavior of the Church at Corinth:

"Your meetings tend to do more harm than good. To begin with, I am told that when you meet as a congregation you fall into sharply divided groups; and I believe there is some truth in it (for dissensions are necessary if only to show which of your members are sound). The result is that when you meet as a congregation, it is impossible for you to eat the Lord's supper, because each of you is in such a hurry to eat his own. And while one goes hungry, another has too much to drink. Have you no homes of your own to eat and drink in? Or are you so contemptuous of the church of God that you shame its poorer members" (1 Cor. 11:17-22)?

Although the behavior St. Paul complains of here is

not described for us in any detail, the basis of his de-
nunciation is evident enough. The Corinthians had
turned the occasion of their eucharistic celebration
into an opportunity for self-indulgence that was fla-
grantly insulting both to their fellow-worshipers and
to the very Lord they worshiped. The irony of the
situation is profound. The Lord's Supper, commem-
oration of that supremely unselfish love whereby
mankind's union with God is achieved, is perverted
into an orgy of selfishness which splits the community into hostile factions mutually forgetful of God
and contemptuous of one another.

Here, surely, is sin. But who is the sinner? It is most
unlikely that any distinct individual could have been
singled out for blame. On the contrary, we seem to
have here an example of that all too familiar kind of
immorality in which a whole social group is impli-
cated, and which could hardly have occurred without their being the social group they are. The sin is
theirs collectively. It is inherent in the very way they
chose to fashion and express their social relationship. The very standard of their sociability was to
make no demands on any love but self-love.

It is easy to imagine how such a thing might happen
in less formal liturgical cirumstances than those we
are most familiar with. (In our churches it happens
in subtler ways.) Affluent early arrivals meet ac-
quaintances of their own class and gravitate together. During a gormandizing *agape* they perhaps
display the quality of their wines by exchanging
samples. Their pleasant meal is made pleasanter by
mutual admiration; they enjoy themselves

thoroughly and—they forget. They forget the less fortunate brethren whose embarrassed reticence under such circumstances would make it even easier than usual to overlook them. And they forget the very meaning of that Lord's Supper at which the only places of honor are reserved—for servants.

Were they surprised, we may wonder, to read the stinging words addressed to them by St. Paul's letter? We can be more confident in giving an affirmative answer to the former question than to the latter one. For a remarkable imperviousness to even the most pointed moral criticism is characteristic of "social sin," mainly for two reasons. First, because the impact of such criticism is subjectively very much weakened by the mere fact of being directed to a whole group! It is as though each one took only a numerical share of the blame, despite the total irrationality of such ethical arithmetic. And second, because social sin is most commonly a sin of omission, and our consciences are notoriously more sensitive to reproach for things we have done than for things we have left undone.

Neither of these attitudes of imperviousness is defensible on the basis of Christian morality. They are, however, so firmly established in our ordinary psychology that they are seldom even subjected to moral criticism. And they combine to form a point of view which powerfully influences a great deal of our moral behavior. That point of view can, perhaps, be stated as a principle, a false principle, more or less as follows: When moral responsibility is perceived as common responsibility, it is evaluated as diminished responsibility.

Let us illustrate this by an example. Suppose that on the street where you live a certain family is in serious straits and badly needs help. Suppose also that you are aware that this family's plight is equally well known to a score of other neighbors, any of whom is as well qualified as yourself to provide the needed help. If no one, in fact, does provide the help, do you not feel less strongly obligated to provide it yourself than you would if nobody else were in a position to do so? Or suppose that the Samaritan in the parable had actually seen the priest and the Levite, and perhaps others as well, pass by the injured victim at the roadside. Would we think it strange if under such circumstances he felt less compunction about passing by himself?

Such reactions come very naturally to most of us, most of the time. And as a result of such reactions it comes about that the more we see others neglect a responsibility which is no less theirs than it is ours, the more easily we neglect it ourselves. Is it not much easier, usually, to ignore a crippled beggar you have just seen a dozen others disregard than it would be if you met him alone?

What is going on in such cases? It looks very much as though a spontaneous mental calculation took place, whereby the strength of the obligation we feel to do something about a given problem is inversely proportional to the number of those who share that same obligation. And if that is the case, it would seem to follow that the more a common obligation *is* neglected, the more likely it is to continue to be neglected. A law of diminishing returns affects the consciences of men in society, and to that law of diminishing returns much of what we know as social sin can certainly be attributed.

I have consistently emphasized that the kind of moral attitude we have been describing and illustrating comes quite naturally to most of us. Moreover, I have little doubt that it can be logically defended on the basis of certain widely respected ethical presuppositions. However that may be, what matters more practically for our present purpose is that it is not the attitude characteristic of Christian ethics. And the fact that it does come to us so naturally may serve as a reminder that Christian morality, despite what many contemporary writers seem to assume, does not come to us in the least naturally.

Perhaps the most direct way to point out the distinctiveness of a Christian ethical response to the kind of situation we have been describing is by recalling the decisive point of view a Christian is called upon to adopt in such cases. For it is not the point of view of one person among many who might provide needed help. Rather, it is the point of view of the person who needs the help. For the Christian's social ethic does not come near being expressed by a determination to "accept your share of social responsibility." It is expressed by a determination to "love your neighbor as yourself." And as a result, when confronted by an instance of human suffering or deprivation, the Christian does not identify himself with the whole group of potential benefactors. He identifies himself with the sufferer. Consequently, the Christian's moral response is determined by how the situation appears from the sufferer's point of view, not from the viewpoint of a collectivity sharing a common obligation. And far from being a mere nicety of ethical theory, this difference of viewpoint is intensely practical in its implications.

Let us return again to that hypothetical neighborhood where everybody knows that one family is desperately in need of help, and where responsibility to provide help falls about equally on all. If we think of ourselves simply as one of the many who share a common responsibility, our sense of obligation is inevitably lessened, and with it our readiness to make any active response. For from that point of view the sufferer is not our special problem. He has no special claim on us individually.

Rather he is a general problem, and has only a general claim on our attention. And for most of us, most of the time, general claims are notoriously weak claims, all too easily forgotten. It would be different if the sufferer were alone with us in his predicament. It would be different if we were the only ones in a position to help. It would be different if he were a special case! Such a reaction is certainly usual. Moreover, it is consistent with its ethical point of view, which is equally usual. It is the ethical point of view of one who sees himself, in his ethical character, as a subject of obligations—sometimes as a unique subject of a special obligation, but other times merely as a partial subject of a general obligation.

Such a point of view is neither unreasonable nor inhuman. But it is un-Christian, and I have already suggested why. Because a strikingly different ethical viewpoint is imposed on Christians precisely by the meaning of the words: "Love your neighbor as yourself." For to love your neighbor as yourself requires that you put yourself in your neighbor's place. But as soon as you do put yourself in your neighbor's place, you are compelled to view the situation very differently, because your ethical viewpoint is now your neighbor's viewpoint—the viewpoint of the one whom you are to love, the viewpoint of the sufferer, of the one in need. And once that viewpoint has been adopted, it is clearly no longer possible to deny that he is a "special case," for who is not a special case from his own viewpoint? What ethical significance can it have from a sufferer's viewpoint that responsibility to assist him in his trouble falls equally upon many? And from his own viewpoint does a sufferer stand less alone and imperative before a potential benefactor when all others ignore him than he would if no others existed?

We remember the way in which a peculiarity of phrasing in our Lord's parable of the good Samaritan brings home to us this contrast of ethical viewpoints. The lawyer had wanted to know: "Who is my neighbor?"—clearly meaning: "Whom am I obliged to love?" Jesus disposed of his particularist viewpoint by telling his story about the two who did nothing to love their fellow countryman and the one who did everything to love a traditionally despicable foreigner. And then, surprisingly, he concluded by asking not "Who was that Samaritan's neighbor?" but rather "Which of these three do you think was neighbor to the man who fell into the hands of the robbers?"

Why this seemingly illogical shift of the lawyer's *status quaestionis* (which has at times received some very strange explanations)? Is it unlikely that what this question was intended to do is what in fact it certainly does do? Namely, forces the questioner to shift his point of view from that of a potential benefactor to that of an actual sufferer. And is it not consistent with the whole orientation of Jesus' moral teaching that he should require such a change of viewpoint? Once again, to understand what it is to love your neighbor as yourself, it is necessary to put yourself in the place of the neighbor who has need of your love.

Imagine yourself in the broken body flung by the roadside, and from that point of view judge what should be done by the passerby! To calculate one's precise share of a common social obligation requires in one's ethical thinking a cool objectivity. To love your neighbor as yourself makes such cool objectivity virtually impossible. And such cool objectivity makes it virtually impossible to love your neighbor as yourself! The contrast here is not between morality and immorality; it is between the morality of Jesus Christ and another morality which most people, including us, find much more comprehensible, practical, and desirable—except on those occasions when we are touched deeply by one of the two things that in this respect can utterly transform our moral viewpoint. Those two things are God's grace, and our own sufferings.

Social sin, I said at the beginning, is not a kind of sin committed by a society. For a society as such cannot sin. A society can kill, but only a human person can commit or condone a murder. A society can deceive, but only a human person can lie. A society can deprive to the point of starvation, but all the greed and all the cruelty must be sought within individual human hearts. In other words, a society can be, for its members or for others outside its membership, an occasion of sin or an instrument of sin. But the sin itself depends on the responses people make to the occasion or the uses people make of the instrument. Among these responses and uses, the possibilities for sin are innumerable; and they continue to multiply with the increasing complexity and diversification of society.

Rather than attempt futilely to list these possibilities, or pointlessly to select among them, I have devoted most of this article to developing a simple but basic thesis that social morality is not precisely the same for Christians as it is, or can be, for others. And because Christian love entails an ethical viewpoint which is essentially inter-subjective, Christians can least of all be justified in leaving urgent social good undone because it is uncertain whose, if anyone's, special obligation it is to do it. And because the greatest contributions to social sin are undoubtedly made not by our sinful actions but by our far more potently sinful inaction, we do well also to recall how characteristically it is sins of omission that the Gospel most resoundingly condemns. Thus on the one occasion when God's final judgment of society is dramatized in the Gospel, we find the negative side of that judgment concerned exclusively with inaction—the food not provided to the hungry, the drink not offered to the thirsty, the clothing not given to the naked, the visits of mercy not made to the suffering and the lonely. Once again the priest and the Levite, now in the form of their pagan and secular counterparts. And on the other side are those who, like the Samaritan, did not ask who was their neighbor, but loved him as themselves, and learned only later and much to their surprise who he was—who he always is.

Chapter 11

The Sacrament Called Penance

The historical background of what we now know as the sacrament of penance is notoriously complicated, and its earliest beginnings are shrouded in obscurity. That obscurity is shared by the famous Matthaean text on binding and loosing, and by its Johannine counterpart on forgiving and retaining sins, to which later theology of the sacrament has so frequently appealed. In the apostolic Church there were evidently differing opinions not only about how, but also about whether serious sins committed after baptism could be remitted. A conviction that they could acquired the status of orthodoxy in opposition to such rigorist heresies as Montanism and Novatianism.

By the third century a recognizable system had taken shape which entailed confession, and a long, arduous period of public penance, preceding readmission to communion. This was certainly no part of the average Christian's life, being a practice reserved for especially heinous sins and permitted only once in a lifetime. In the fourth and fifth centuries, when the matter was often treated by ecclesiastical writers, this system was prevalent in both the East and the West, and the "order of penitents" comprised those for whom fulfilling its requirements constituted virtually a way of life. On the other hand, there is no convincing evidence that private confession and absolution was a recognized procedure. "Ordinary" sins were dealt with by the personal penances of individuals, assisted at times by salutary exhortation or rebuke on the part of the clergy.

The physically rigorous and socially humiliating character of the early public penitential system inevitably intimidated all but the most highly motivated penitents, and it was therefore commonly postponed until death seemed imminent. The successor to this rather unsuccessful system was introduced by sixth-century monastic missionaries of the British Isles, and was based on their new invention of the "Penitential Books." These volumes were compendia of prayers to be said, questions to be asked, and penances to be prescribed by confessors in private interviews with repentant sinners. The penances were at first protracted and severe. In the course of time, however, they became gentler, and allowed the substitution of prayers or almsgiving in lieu of corporal austerities. The logic of this development implied, of course, a kind of exchange rate, whereby so many days of austerity could be equated with so many prayers recited or so much money contributed. And a further extension of this notion of practical equivalencies gave rise to the much-misunderstood and much-abused numerical and financial aspects of the doctrine of indulgences, which proved so damagingly scandalous at the time of the Reformation. At the same time, since the Penitential Books served as confessors' manuals, indicating proportionate penances for particular sins, their development and popularity contributed greatly to that almost obsessive concern with classifying and rating sins which became so characteristic of Catholic moral theology.

Once the system we have been describing was modified to the extent of conceding absolution when an assigned penance had been accepted, instead of after it was completed, the basic design of the modern private penance system was established. It was basically this system which was presupposed by the Fourth Lateran Council's decree imposing the obligation of annual confession. And it was also the system envisioned by the medieval schoolmen, especially St. Thomas, whose teaching concerning this sacrament became the accepted theology of post-Reformation Catholicism.

At the moment, it is evident to even the most casual observer of what Roman Catholics have been saying and doing, that the sacrament of penance has come on uneasy times. It seems hardly likely that it will mean or do for my children's generation of Catholics precisely what it meant and did for their grandparents; and it is no longer an idle question to ask if it is likely to mean anything at all to my children's generation. As things are going at present, it is perfectly conceivable that Catholics now alive may in a very few years find literary allusions to "confessors" as alien to their experience as references to the "pardoner" in Chaucer's *Canterbury Tales.*

Awareness that a kind of rapid obsolescence seems to be affecting the long-established understanding and practice of the sacrament of penance has already elicited numerous plans for remodeling it along more congenial lines. Nearly all of these projects are strongly influenced by a desire to personalize and socialize the sacrament, corresponding to a widely shared conviction that for a long time it has been far too impersonal and individualistic. As tokens of this attitude, we increasingly find the old confessional "box," with its atmosphere of formality, secrecy, anonymity, and isolation, giving way to the format either of a candid and sympathetic counseling interview in surroundings conducive to affability, or of a communal celebration of public liturgy designed to express a collective acknowledgment of sinfulness and common assurance of forgiveness.

It is no part of my purpose in this article to criticize these pastoral and liturgical efforts, which are in general both respectful of important traditions and sensitive to important actualities. Still less is it my purpose to add to or improve upon them. Instead, I wish to suggest that in the course of its eventful history the sacrament of penance has accumulated a variety of aspects, implications, and associations which have never been either satisfactorily integrated or critically sorted out. And I believe this to be an important part of what is wrong with the sacrament of penance. A sacrament is a sign, a vehicle of meaning. And in the case of penance, the meaning has become confused, and the sign is therefore confusing.

Take, for example, the very name of the sacrament. Is penance a good label? Does it point to what this sacrament is understood to mean as a sign, or what it is believed to accomplish as an instrument of grace? It certainly does not identify the action of God, the grace of the sacrament. But neither does it identify the symbolic human action which manifests that grace. And what is more, for contemporary Christians it does not even refer to a feature of the sacrament which, as they understand and experience it, is at all prominent or expressive.

For the modern Catholic, penance enters into the sacrament only as a rather trivial epilogue consisting in the recitation of a few vocal prayers or, with more imaginative confessors, performing some good deed more or less appropriate to one's ethical situation. And as a result, the sacrament has long been popularly designated by the feature which does stand out in most people's experience of it: confession. And indeed, confession has probably been for most modern Catholics what penance was for early Christians, the most impressive and memorable aspect of this sacrament because it is the most intimidating and uncomfortable.

No doubt a great deal of effort has been put forth in recent years by enlightened pastors to bring about a less confession-centered approach to the sacrament of penance. Such efforts will be fully successful only when neither ministers nor recipients of this sacrament are any longer haunted by the unfortunate legacy of what began with the Penitential Books: moral theology's doctrinaire taxonomy of sin, with its vast accumulated catalogues of *peccata ex genere suo mortalia.* For the penitent who feels called upon to compare his moral record with this vaguely comprehended list of "intrinsically grievous" sins, and then weigh subjective dispositions and extenuating circumstances to determine what he is obliged to confess, can scarcely avoid a confession-centered approach which is neither religiously significant, nor ethically productive, nor psychologically healthy. But that raises a further question. For if neither spiritual nor ethical nor psychological interests are promoted by this kind of confessional self-scrutiny, is there any other relevant perspective which might seem more favorable to such a procedure? And of course there is. And that perspective, which has influenced the sacrament of penance throughout its entire history, brings to view what is usually called its juridical aspect.

The juridical aspect of penance is certainly nothing new. As we have seen, the earliest recognizable form of this sacrament had a decidedly juridical complexion, being a system whereby the early Church, having judged the gravity of a confessed (and usually public) offense, passed sentence upon the offender, after which the latter "served his term" in what can certainly be described as a "penal institution." All of this was, of course, to prepare the offender for readmission to communion, and the penitential ordeal was expected to serve the multiple purpose of punishing the offender, contributing to his moral rehabilitation, and assuring the Church of the genuineness and reliability of his reform.

The resemblance of all this to familiar patterns of secular penal justice is both obvious and significant. And part of its significance should remind us that this early usage was strongly influenced by consideration of the sinner's alienation from the visible Church, the society of his fellow-Christians. It was therefore shaped by a point of view which saw the sinner as a kind of "enemy of the people," whose reintegration into their community must be carefully prepared for, as much in the interest of the community itself as for his own spiritual healing. In other words, we do not find in the early penitential discipline a sharp distinction between sins committed against God and crimes committed against the society of the Church: between *peccata* and *delicta*.

Consequently, in the "order of penitents,' the status of a sinner is scarcely distinguishable from that of an excommunicate, and the conditions of absolution from sin are closely linked, both in thought and in practice, with what we should call the requirements for a lifting of censure. Of course, even in modern confessional discipline we find a formula of absolution which includes, though not indiscriminately, both sins and censures. And we still hear the confessor's role described as *simul medicus et iudex*, both that of a healer and that of a magistrate.

The two matters we have just discussed, the appropriateness of the name penance, and the combination of juridical and moral aspects of the sacrament, can be usefully related on the basis of a little elementary word study. For if you look up the word *poenitentia* in a classical Latin dictionary (*Cassell's* is the one I checked), you do not find it rendered into English as "penance," but as "repentance, penitence." And if you then look up "penance" in the same dictionary, you find it translated into Latin as *satisfactio, mulcta*, and *poena*. The contrast is highly significant. For whereas the former set of words describes a moral and psychological disposition of mind, the other refers to something very different, the discharge of a legal penalty. The former is a condition achieved by conscience, whereas the latter is a condition imposed by law. And to bring in one more bit of relevant philology, we may also observe that the classical Latin sense of *poenitentia* is not at all remote from that of the Greek word *metanoia* in the New Testament, whereas the meaning of our English word "penance" is very remote from it indeed.

The point of this linguistic excursion is not, of course, simply to call for a reform of vocabulary. It is to suggest that confusing developments in the language of penance have as more serious counterparts confusing developments in the theology of penance. For what gets confused in both cases is the moral with the juridical realm. Thus penitence becomes confused with penalty. Thus a sin against God becomes confused with a crime against Christian society. And thus forgiveness of sin becomes confused with absolution of censure. I do not, of course, mean that these things are confused in the minds of competent theologians or of theologically educated clergy and laity. But they are deeply confused in popular understanding; they have long been confused in Christian culture, and the history of their confusion is deeply inscribed in the evolution of the sacrament of penance.

I personally find it very difficult to believe that the sacrament of penance will be employed to the best spiritual advantage of Christians until or unless its moral and juridical strands are decisively untangled, and not only in theory but in lucid symbolic expression. The "physician" and the "judge" must, I think, be made to occupy separate offices, so to speak, if the faithful are ever to know clearly where they are and what they are doing, and what is being done to them! But I do not pretend that a liturgical reform along these lines can be put through immediately, or casually, or without careful and difficult theological, historical, and pastoral preparation. And if it should be decided that a real sacrament of penance is altogether detachable from the exercise of "jurisdiction," the ecclesiological consequences would no doubt be far-reaching.

Meanwhile, even if I am right in believing that official doctrine and official discipline with respect to the sacrament of penance perpetuate a lot of avoidable confusion, the actual situation is neither stagnant nor hopeless. Increasingly, the juridical and moral aspects are being sorted out at least in the minds of many confessors and penitents themselves, and for the most part this sorting out results in a de-emphasis almost to the vanishing point of the juridical features of the sacrament. At the same time, the heightened liturgical sensibility of modern Catholics encourages them to think of this sacrament as an act of worship and an expression of the grace of God. On this foundation, the sacrament can be made helpful and intelligible, and therefore acceptable, to modern Christians even without a thoroughgoing official reform, merely by playing up certain existing elements and playing down others.

St. Thomas established the distinction of three elements in a patient's participation in this sacrament: contrition, confession, and satisfaction. Of these elements, the first is a personal, moral, and religious act, which is obviously a basic predisposition for forgiveness. Correctly perceived, it is an inner conversion or change of heart (*metanoia*), which as far as possible repudiates sin as an orientation of life which estranges one from and opposes one to the love of God and neighbor. When not confused with merely emotional guilt feelings or disappointed self-esteem, it is an experience whose moral value is transformed into religious value by faith in the mercy of God.

The second element, confession, can be viewed in two very different ways. The first is closely connected with contrition and sees it as a frank admission and humble confrontation of that sinful direction of life which makes it both alien and hostile to God and man. The alternative way of viewing confession is plainly juridical, seeing it as a scrupulous deposition of testimony before a tribunal as prerequisite to judgment. That this sort of thing is important for the efficient administration of human justice is obvious; but what it has to do with the bestowal of divine mercy is by no means obvious.

Finally, satisfaction (as distinct from reform or amendment of life) is not only an entirely juridical notion, but is based on a conception of retributive justice whose philosophical soundness is highly questionable and has been too long taken for granted: the idea that retribution, or "vindictive penalty" is intrinsically valuable as somehow "restoring the order of justice" or "paying one's debt to society." Whether such thinking originates in the appreciation of justice or in the rationalization of vengeance is a question that has gone too long unanswered. But however it is answered, the relevance of retribution to the Christian conception of a boundlessly forgiving God would seem difficult indeed to establish.

A sacrament is a sign of grace. A courtroom trial is not. Forgiveness is an act of grace. Legal judgment is not. The grace of the sacrament of penance is forgiveness, and this alone is what the sacrament as a visible sign is meant to convey. Nothing else has to be included; and nothing which detracts from that should be included. The atmosphere of the sacrament of penance should take its cue not from the sober and careful proceedings of even the most enlightened tribunals, for a tribunal is simply not the place to go for forgiveness. Its atmosphere should be derived, as purely as it can be derived, from the abundant Gospel imagery of a boundlessly forgiving, inexhaustibly loving God. Our celebration of the sacramental liturgy of forgiveness should be worthy of the father of the prodigal son. Far too often in the past, it has rather expressed the attitude of his elder brother.

Chapter 12

Growing Up Moral

Unless things change very greatly during the next twenty-five years, the present century is unlikely to be celebrated by intellectual historians as one in which either philosophy or theology made any remarkable contribution to the subject of ethics. There is a better chance, however, that the century will be credited with a major impact on ethical thought derived from the social sciences, and especially from psychology. For although empirical scientific study of moral thought and behavior has been pursued for only a short time and by few investigators, it has already produced impressive results in the form of theories supported by considerable data.

While these results are not, for the most part, explicitly related to theology, the intimate relationship which exists in Christianity between religion and morals makes this material highly relevant to the study of Christian ethics or moral theology. The purpose of this article, therefore, will be to call attention to some characteristic findings of recent research in the psychology of morality and to suggest that they deserve serious consideration by

any who have special interest in either ethical
theory or moral formation.

To limit so vast a subject, I shall concentrate on the
normal maturation of moral thinking—what some
might call the evolution of an adult conscience. In
dealing with this topic, I shall be mainly
summarizing (and, inevitably, grossly
oversimplifying) some of the findings of the great
Swiss psychologist, Jean Piaget, and of his American
successor in this area of research, Lawrence
Kohlberg. Lack of space will prevent me from saying
much about the areas of disagreement between
these two men, and from comparing their work with
older alternative theories such as psychoanalytic
accounts of superego formation, or behaviorist
explanations based on conditioned learning. The
following account, therefore, is admittedly both
superficial and selective; its purpose will be best
served if it encourages the reading of more
adequate material.

In all civilizations it is commonly assumed that moral
judgment, like other kinds of judgment, is a
function of age and experience. Kinds of moral
thinking which we consider normal and acceptable
in young children, we tend to regard as disgraceful
and intolerable in a grown man or woman. We take
for granted, in other words, that there are moral
aspects to growing up. We do not suppose that
ethical maturity is automatically and inevitably
achieved, for it is all too clear that arrested
development and delayed development are as
possible in moral mentalities as in other dimensions

of mental life. In other words, time and experience are considered necessary conditions, but not' sufficient ones, for the emergence in adulthood of morally mature thinking.

An important aspect of psychological research pertaining to ethics has been its attempt to trace a normal pattern in the development of moral judgment, indicate the outstanding phases of its growth, and relate these to the kinds of experience which characteristically influence them. Before reviewing some of these findings, it should be noted that what we are chiefly concerned with is moral judgment, as distinct from moral conduct; we do not wish to beg the question of whether a free will can choose behavior which is clearly judged to be morally wrong. And since in Catholic moral theology conscience has generally been defined as moral judgment, we are in that sense concerned with the development of conscience, without denying that even with a mature conscience one can refuse to act conscientiously.

Piaget's research points in general to the existence of two distinct levels of moral development. The first level, characteristic of young children, tends as they grow older to be gradually replaced by the second. This replacement often does not take place completely, and it may not take place at all. Consequently, the first level may be found rather purely exemplified in young children; with older persons the picture is less simple and may be expected to combine, in various proportions, traits characteristic of the two stages. What these traits are can best be illustrated in connection with three areas of investigation: first, the conception of rules; second, the basis of moral judgment; third, the interpretation of punishment.

With regard to the conception of rules, Piaget drew very interesting conclusions from systematically observing and inquiring about the way rules are employed in children's games—rules which are, of course, much freer than most from adult intervention and enforcement. The most striking discovery in this area of investigation was that young children typically regard the rules of their games as deriving from the authority of some decidedly superior beings, whether older children, or adults, or even God himself. Consistent with this view of the origin of rules was the children's further conviction that the rules are immutable and inviolable. Changing the rules seemed to them strictly unthinkable, and breaking rules was assumed to be inexcusable.

However, as the children grow older, they come to look on the rules very differently. They are seen as human inventions, presumably designed for the games by players themselves. Consequently, the rules can be changed when a change would clearly be advantageous to the game. Since, however, the function of rules is to facilitate mutual participation in the game, to change them is assumed to require mutual agreement by the players. Interestingly, the younger children, whose view of the rules was characteristically so strict, were found to violate them with the utmost nonchalance, whereas the older children, with their much more flexible conception of the rules, were much more conscientious about observing them.

In the area of moral judgment, differences between the criteria employed by younger and older children were found to be equally pronounced. Younger children, for example, typically attach little or no importance to the intention of one who violates a recognized rule of conduct; whether the infraction is deliberate or not simply does not matter. What does matter in assessing the gravity of a violation is the magnitude of its consequences: either the damage which results or the punishment which follows or the importance of the persons who are offended. In contrast, older children attribute great importance to intention. Harm which is done indeliberately is not considered blameworthy, whereas deliberate malice even in small matters is strongly disapproved. Likewise, the deliberate violation of accepted standards of behavior is considered equally reprehensible regardless of the status of the persons offended, and of whether or not punishment ensues.

Punishment itself exhibits great discrepancy of meaning between the two levels. The younger children regard punishment as an indispensable and even an inevitable consequence of rule-breaking. No thought is given to the appropriateness of punishment but only to its intensity, and there is a tendency to assume that more punishment is always better than less. In keeping with this view, punishment is clearly understood as expiatory, as "paying the price" of one's misdeeds, rather than as a corrective or salutary measure. For the innocent associates of offenders to suffer punishment along with them is readily accepted. Moreover, a close, almost automatic connection between infraction and retribution can be seen in the children's tendency to interpret as punishment any mishap, however coincidental, which occurs after wrongdoing.

Among older children, on the other hand, punishment is typically regarded as a corrective measure and is evaluated accordingly. It is therefore assumed that punishment should as far as possible "fit the crime," and therapy serve more usefully as an instrument of reform. By the same token, when it is evident that a violator has already genuinely reformed, it is understood that punishment can be dispensed with altogether.

In his interpretation of these and similar findings, Piaget characterizes the moral mentality of early childhood as "moral realism." By this he means that the domain of right and wrong is perceived as absolute, as extrinsic to the individual, as unaffected by circumstances, and as consisting of rigid norms imposed by unassailable authority. At a more mature level, this gives way to a "morality of reciprocity," in which obligations are understood to be rooted in social relationships and to be valuable insofar as they insure mutual benefit in shared undertakings.

Transition from the immature to the mature level of

moral thinking is attributed to two basic factors, one developmental and the other social. The developmental factor is an aspect of mental growth. It consists in acquiring the capacity to enter into the viewpoints of persons other than oneself, which Piaget describes as passing from "egocentric" to "operational" thinking. The social factor, clearly related to the developmental one, is the transition from functioning always as a subordinate of superiors—a child in an adult-regulated world—to assuming the role of one who collaborates with his peers in planning and carrying out common enterprises.

Since Piaget's findings were published more than forty years ago, the most outstanding continuator of his work on the development of moral judgment has been Kohlberg. Although essentially within the tradition of his Swiss predecessor, Kohlberg's theory concentrates on developmental factors to the exclusion of social ones, and presents a general picture which comprises three levels of maturation in moral thinking. At each of these levels, he further distinguishes two different stages.

The lowest level, called preconventional, is one at which children accept the moral rules and evaluations given to them, but do so merely on the basis of avoiding pain and seeking pleasure. At the earlier stage of this level, physical consequences are the sole decisive factor, while at a slightly higher stage the satisfaction of one's needs becomes a dominant influence.

The second level is labeled conventional, for it is ruled by conformity with the expectations and demands of one's society. At the earlier stage corresponding to this level, the major motive is eagerness to please others. At the later stage this is replaced by a more generally dutiful attitude toward authorities and regulations.

The third and highest level, which is described as post-conventional or principled, is characterized by adherence to principles and values independently of their sponsorship by society and authority. The lower stage of this level is characterized by an emphasis on individual rights and a legal-contractual approach to problems of preserving those rights among the diversified standards found within society. Finally, at the highest stage in this scheme (which, according to recent statements by Kohlberg, may not be the highest of all), what is right is determined by personal moral decision in accordance with abstract ethical principles which have been freely adopted.

Psychological investigations and their results, such as the ones we have just outlined, deserve a great deal more attention than they currently receive from persons concerned with imparting moral education and upholding moral standards. These include not only ethicians and moral theologians, but parents, teachers, and clergy. For while there is undoubtedly a danger of accepting and applying such theories in an uncritical and doctrinaire manner, it would be most unwise simply to ignore such significant data and plausible interpretations as they have brought to our attention. Without attempting any detailed evaluation of this material, we may note a few practical implications.

The most general conclusion which these psychological findings impose upon us is that human thinking about moral issues exhibits a complex pattern of development in the course of human life. Even allowing for an abundance of error and exaggeration, psychology must be credited with having shown convincingly that mature and immature moral judgments differ profoundly and rest on very different bases. Moreover, the changes which characteristically take place in moral judgment are not simply produced by instruction and example, but emerge gradually in the course of mental growth.

Perhaps the most important inference to be drawn from this is that elders or superiors, who persist in imposing moral lessons and moral obligations on their dependents in a rigid manner which takes no account of development and diversity, are acting unnaturally and unreasonably. Yet this is, of course, done by countless people nearly all the time, with the result that individuals whose moral judgment is decidedly mature find themselves subjected to kinds of moralizing that are appropriate to infantile levels of development.

Young persons, for example, whose moral judgment is firmly based on freely adopted principles, regularly find themselves, in family, educational, political, and religious life, presented with crassly punitive motives and shallowly conformist ideologies. That they should be alienated by such experience is inevitable, for to require mature judgment to submit to childish standards is extremely offensive in any area of life and especially so in the realm of morality.

It might also be noted in this context that religious and theological teachings frequently embody moral judgments, and as some of these teachings are often presented, the moral judgments they embody are scarcely typical of maturity in ethical thinking. How often, for example, are virtually all the rules commended by religion, from the broadest principles to the most trivial stipulations, presented as though they were arbitrary and immutable decrees of unexceptionable divine authority? How often is the seriousness of moral delinquency expressed largely or entirely with reference to the intensity and duration of punishment established for it? How often have the consequences of personal sin been described in the most crudely expiatory terms of penalties incurred?

How often has even our redemption by Christ been interpreted as a kind of satisfaction for sin which seems to imply a rather primitive ethical mentality in God himself? How often have the doctrines, both of atonement and of original sin, implied a less than admirable divine complacency and complicity in causing the innocent to suffer what only the guilty deserve? How often have Christian people been encouraged to respond to ecclesiastical authority with an uncritically literal subservience whose

rationale must be sought at the most immature
levels of moral judgment?

It is, I think, high time that preachers of religion and
teachers of theology took very seriously the fact that
some of their teachings are judged to be ethically
absurd by standards which seem precisely
characteristic of mature moral judgment. It is, of
course, perfectly possible in such cases that the
doctrines are misunderstood or misrepresented, or
that shallow minds mistake profundity for absurdity.
But it is nonetheless true that doctrinal formulations
which seem unworthy of the moral judgment of
mature human minds need at least to be carefully
reexamined and clearly elucidated. It is sadly true
that a great many conscientious people have been
repelled by the moral implications of religious
teachings, because they found them not too lofty or
demanding, but too primitive or puerile. While such
judgments may, of course, be arrogant, it is equally
arrogant automatically to assume that they are.

This whole subject is especially important at a time
when Christians are increasingly urged to "rely on
their own consciences" in resolving moral issues.
For if what is meant here by "conscience" is nothing
more than an irrational feeling of rightness or
wrongness associated with a certain kind of
behavior, then to advise people to rely on it is highly
irresponsible. But if, on the other hand, conscience
is understood to mean moral judgment, then we
ought clearly to recognize that like all other kinds of
judgment it is not uniformly reliable. In moral
matters as in all serious matters, the only kind of

judgment that we can confidently rely on is mature judgment. And in moral matters as in other serious matters, we need all the information we can get about what mature judgment really consists in, how to identify it, foster its development, and encourage its exercise.

Suggested Readings

Chapter 1

For an argument maintaining that neither the natural law nor the teaching authority of the Church necessitates insisting on absolute norms in moral theology, see: Charles E. Curran, *A New Look at Christian Morality* (Notre Dame: Fides, 1970), ch. 3. For indications of just how new the so-called new morality really is, see: John G. Milhaven, *Toward a New Catholic Morality* (Garden City: Doubleday, 1970), ch. 1 and 9. For a warning against the consequences of shallow and simplistic love ethics, see: Stanley Hauerwas, "Love's Not All You Need," *Cross Currents 22* (1972) 225-237, available as a separate reprint. James Gustafson's *Christian Ethics and the Community* (Philadelphia: Pilgrim, 1971), ch. 3, offers an excellent discussion under the title "Context Versus Principles: A Misplaced Debate in Christian Ethics." A helpful Catholic reference in this connection is Richard A. McCormick's *Ambiguity in Moral Choice* (Milwaukee: Marquette, 1973).

Chapter 2

For a general criticism of Catholic moral theology's treatment of sexuality, including a review of recent developments, see Charles E. Curran, *Contemporary Problems in Moral Theology* (Notre Dame:

Fides, 1970), ch. 3. And on the flexibility of Catholic doctrine with regard to absolute norms derived from natural law, see the same author's *A New Look at Christian Morality* (Notre Dame: Fides, 1968), ch. 3, 8. For a clear differentiation of sexual love from distinctively Christian love, and a discussion of their relationship, see C.S. Lewis, *The Four Loves* (London: Fontana), ch. 3, 4. A Christian evaluation of sexual behavior in the light of personal and conjugal values is presented by Peter A. Bertocci, *Sex, Love, and the Person* (New York: Sheed and Ward, 1967), especially ch. 5.

Chapter 3

Virtually all aspects of the abortion question are treated by experts in the appropriate fields in Robert E. Cooke (ed.), *The Terrible Choice: The Abortion Dilemma* (N.Y.: Bantam, 1968). For historical perspective, a very valuable contribution is John T. Noonan, *The Morality of Abortion* (Cambridge: Harvard, 1970). Some brief but helpful remarks on desirable modifications in the treatment of abortion by Catholic moral theology are furnished by Charles E. Curran, *A New Look at Christian Morality* (Notre Dame: Fides, 1970), pp. 237ff.

Chapter 4

For a clear, brief, balanced, and wise Christian perspective on marriage, I know of no more recent book that improves on Dietrich Von Hildebrand's *Marriage* (New York: Sheed & Ward, 1948). A more personalistic and psychological approach to the subject is Eugene Kennedy's *What a Modern Catholic Believes about Marriage* (Chicago: Thomas More, 1972). The definitive study of Catholic tradition on the morality of birth control procedures is John. T. Noonan's *Contraception* (New York: Mentor-Omega, 1965). A thorough critique of the natural law implications of Pope Paul VI's doctrine in *Humanae Vitae* is provided by Charles E. Curran's *Contemporary Problems in Moral Theology* (Notre Dame: Fides, 1970), ch. 2.

Chapter 5

A useful contribution to the re-evaluation of divorce that is currently being carried out by American Catholics is V.J. Pospishil's *Divorce and Remarriage: Towards a New Catholic Teaching* (New York: Herder & Herder, 1967). An entire number of *Commonweal* (April 14, 1967) devoted to the subject offers a good sampling of liberal views. A useful recent article which may be made available in reprint is William B. Curtin's "The Dilemma of Second Marriages" in *America* (August 18, 1973). An excellent brief introduction to the idea that what Jesus gives us is "not law but Gospel" is Joachim Jeremias' *The Sermon on the Mount* (Philadelphia: Fortress, 1963), which ought to be accompanied by good modern commentaries on the New Testament texts concerning divorce.

Chapter 6

Although the literature on prejudice is enormous, I would single out the volume from which I quoted above, Gordon W. Allport's *The Nature of Prejudice* (Garden City: Doubleday, 1958), and especially its chapter 28, on "Religion and Prejudice." The distinction employed there between two radically different kinds of religion is further developed in Allport's *The Individual and His Religion* (New York: Macmillan, 1950). As a clear statement of the basic Christian view of God of which Christian love is the moral realization, I recommend Joachim Jeremias' *The Central Message of the New Testament* (New York: Scribner's, 1965). For a more speculative account of the relationship between love of God and love of neighbor, Karl Rahner's "Reflections on the Unity of the Love of Neighbor and the Love of God" in the 6th volume of his *Theological Investigations* (Baltimore: Helicon, 1969) may prove helpful.

Chapter 7

The Road to H: Narcotics, Delinquency, and Social Policy, by Isidore Chein et al. (New York: Basic Books, 1964), although written almost a decade ago and concerned primarily with heroin use, is a study which has acquired the reputation of a minor classic, and whose perspective is relevant to the whole contemporary drug problem. *Marijuana and Social Evolution*, by J.S. Hochman (Englewood Cliffs: Prentice Hall, 1972) is an excellent survey of its subject in a more than usually broad frame of reference. For a more personal and compassionate appreciation of the dynamics of addiction and recovery, *We Were Hooked*, edited by Harold Flender (New York: Random House, 1972) offers thirteen autobiographical case histories which are both typical and poignantly individual.

Chapter 8

Two interesting recent studies of dishonesty in our society, which suggest that, even from a purely secular and pragmatic viewpoint, it has become dangerously excessive, are Carl J. Friedrich's *The Pathology of Politics* (New York: Harper & Row, 1972), and Mark Lipman's *Stealing* (New York: Harper & Row, 1973). A number of thought-provoking reflections on the same subject in an ecclesiastical context are provided in Hans Küng's *Truthfulness: The Future of the Church* (New York: Sheed & Ward, 1968). A balanced approach to the question of the New Testament's relevance to secular ethical issues can be found in Rudolf Schnackenburg's *The Moral Teaching of the New Testament* (New York: Seabury, 1973), especially chapter 4.

Chapter 9

Sex: Thoughts for Contemporary Christians, edited by Michael Taylor (New York: Doubleday, 1972) contains two helpful articles on a specifically Christian attitude toward homosexuality, one from a subjective viewpoint by a homosexual, and the other from an objective point of view by a theologian.

Jack Dominian, a British psychiatrist, gives an enlightened account of his profession's still very limited understanding of homosexuality in *Psychiatry and the Christian* (New York: Hawthorn, 1962), ch. 5. A typical "new morality" perspective on homosexuality is represented by J.G. Milhaven's *Towards a New Catholic Morality* (New York: Doubleday, 1970), Ch. 4.

Chapter 10

An interesting recent book by an outstanding psychiatrist, which urges the importance of preserving the idea of sin in our thinking about social problems, is Karl Menninger's *Whatever Became of Sin?* (New York: Hawthorn, 1973). James M. Gustafson's *Christian Ethics and the Community* (Philadelphia: Pilgrim, 1971) is an explicitly Protestant essay on social morality which stresses inter-subjectivity and de-emphasizes the sense of obligation. A very brief and very basic statement on Christian social ethics, which emphasizes their inseparability from Christian religious convictions, is the chapter on "Social Morality" in C.S. Lewis' *Mere Christianity* (New York: Macmillan, 1960).

Chapter 11

Helpful reflections on the present situation of the sacrament of penance in both pastoral practice and theological interpretation are provided by Charles Curran's "The Sacrament of Penance Today," in *Contemporary Problems in Moral Theology* (Notre

Dame: Fides, 1970). The same writer's "Conversion: The Central Moral Message of Jesus," in *A New Look at Christian Morality* (Notre Dame: Fides, 1970) contains useful observations on the nature of repentance. John Gallen's "General Sacramental Absolution: Pastoral Remarks on Pastoral Norms," *Theological Studies* (1973) is an aid to interpreting and using the present discipline of the Church for general absolution in penance services. Vincent Taylor's *Forgiveness and Reconciliation* (London: Macmillan, 1941) remains, I think, the best thing we have in English on the New Testament theology of forgiveness and what follows from forgiveness.

Chapter 12

The pioneering classic in this field, which has the added merit of being a very readable book, is Jean Piaget's *The Moral Judgment of the Child* (New York: Collier, 1962). Lawrence Kohlberg gives an excellent summary of his own findings, and discusses their implications for moral training and teaching in *Moral Education: Interdisciplinary Approaches*, edited by C.M. Beck, B.S. Crittenden, and E.V. Sullivan (New York: Newman, 1971). A very helpful survey of the whole field of psychological aspects of morality is provided by Derek Wright's *The Psychology of Moral Behavior* (Baltimore: Penguin, 1971).